That's O.K. God!

By

Mary Virostek

Rainbow's End Company
354 Golden Grove Road
Baden, Pennsylvania 15005

"Behold, I will do a new thing; now it shall spring forth, shall ye not know it?"
Isaiah 43:19

Copyright © 1991

by

Mary Virostek

All rights reserved. No material in this book may be copied, reproduced, or used in any way without permission in writing from the publisher.

ISBN: 0-9608780-5-X

Written in collaboration with
Bettie Corbin Tucker and Wayne P. Brumagin

Edited by Judith Blanarik

Scripture quotations are taken from
THE LIVING BIBLE, Tyndale House
Publishers, Wheaton, Illinois

DEDICATION

To --

Nicole, our granddaughter, whose contagious smile, trusting attitude, and innocent outlook softens the hearts of many.

Don and Nicole enjoyed working in the garden together, planting seeds and harvesting the fruit of their labor. During their short time together, her "Pap Pap," through words and actions, sowed seeds of faith and understanding in her young mind. These seeds will last a lifetime, with God gathering the yield from the harvest.

FOREWORD

As I read Mary's story, or shall I say, her three stories in one -- Don's, Mary's and the Lord's, a memory reentered . . .

I had a conversation with Mary and Don in which he gave witness to his firmly grounded faith and his belief that God could indeed heal him. I left the hospital room confused. I knew that the medical prognosis pointed to the strong possibility that he would not survive. Then there was Don's faith and the Christian tradition which has, throughout history, surprised and overruled the best that science and medicine have sometimes nationally claimed and predicted. As a person and chaplain I was torn. Medicine and religion; doubt and faith; hope and fear were again all at crossroads. Yet, in my years of hospital experience and ministry, I had seen the curtain of death pulled too many times to rest comfortably with an assurance that Don would beat the medical odds and be healed. I also had come to believe that even though Paul says that death is the enemy in our relationship to God, death itself could be a healing -- a release which enables a whole restoration of the person to God.

I began to realize that it wasn't necessary for me to somehow convince Don that he might not be healed here on earth. With his faith, in his own time, he would know. As he said, "I guess I'm willing to get on the 'train' to Heaven and be with the Lord." Then there was Don's loving admonition to Mary, telling her that he hoped she might re-marry. Whether or not this ever happened, it was a clear message from Don that he knew he would die. I did not need to *"prepare"* Don.

I surmised that I needed to *walk* with Mary and be a part of the fellowship which surrounded her. My contribution was to help her face the denial, and the acceptance of Don's illness and destiny. When talking with me, Mary was open with her feelings and thoughts. She was willing to trust me -- and others -- to walk with her as she painfully lived those days of hope, fear and pain. Mary's deep and sensitive faith has truly been wrought out of medical and human mire and darkness which occurs, or can occur, as bad things happen to good people.

Mary has subsequently wrestled with her grief, and through the process, continues to realize that she is a woman in her own right. She is a woman who is capable of giving voice -- not only to her beloved husband -- but to her heart and soul. Her voice is one of sincerity, integrity, and simplicity; it is laced with human honesty. She represents *human beings*, enabling them to give voice to their experiences of life, death, and grief. Mary has given witness that she is a spokesperson for what the life, suffering, death, and resurrection of Jesus Christ means for we who are created human.

Reverend Phil W. Williams
Chaplain, West Penn Hospital

INTRODUCTION

This book has been written with the intent of helping those who have gone through, or are going through, the loss of a loved one. It is my prayer that it will minister to those separated from loved ones through death, divorce, or confinement in a prison or nursing home. Perhaps a family member has run away or moved to a distant place. In all of these situations, there is a sense of emptiness and loneliness -- a need for answers!

Throughout Don's illness, I lived one moment at a time, relying on Christ for strength. There were times when I was angry with God for not miraculously and instantly curing my husband of cancer. This has left me with unanswered questions, but I can truly say, "That's okay, God -- I trust you in all situations."

After Don's death, I struggled for individual independence and identity. The grief process is also a growth process which freed me from living in the past and led me to ultimate victory in Jesus. You, too, can have this victory and live a productive and fulfilling life in accordance with God's plans.

As you read these words, my prayer for you is found in Ephesians 3:17-20:

> *And I pray that Christ will be more at home in your hearts, living within you as you trust in Him. May your roots go down deep into the soil of God's marvelous love and may you be able to feel and understand, as all God's children should, how long, how wide, how deep, and how high His love really is; and to experience this love for yourselves, though it is so great that you will never see the end of it or fully know or understand it. And so at last you will be filled up with God himself.*

Now glory be to God who by His mighty power at work within us is able to do far more than we would ever dare to ask or even dream of -- infinitely beyond our highest prayers, desires, thoughts, or hopes.

CONTENTS

Beginnings 15

I, Mary, Take Thee, Don 21

Growing Together 27

Jesus -- Lord of Our Lives 33

In Sickness and In Health 43

Community of Angels 53

A Letter to Jesus 63

The Train to Heaven 67

Why? 75

Preparations 81

Tunnel of Grieving 85

A Victorious Landing 93

About Don Virostek 99

1

BEGINNINGS

"Dying isn't so hard. It's leaving you that's going to be so difficult."

My husband Don had spoken these loving, but agonizing words to me only a few weeks earlier when the doctor told us that he had only a month to live. Formerly one of the top basketball players at the University of Pittsburgh, he was now reduced to being an invalid, a paraplegic confined to a hospital bed. As his breathing became more and more labored, and the cancer continued its ravaging destruction, I found myself crying out again to God. "Please, please," I begged. "Help me -- help us -- this can't be happening!"

Apprehensively, I summoned the nurse. "He's worse," I said, swallowing nervously. "Should -- should I call our kids?"

I watched her reaction, desperately wanting her to say that it wouldn't be necessary -- not yet.

Her eyes met mine and I saw sympathy. "Yes," she said softly. "Mrs. Virostek, it's time to call them."

A part of me wanted to scream out in protest -- in anger -- in frustration, but, instead, I gently reached for Don's hand. "I love you," I said looking down at the man I had married more than a quarter of a century before. This frail, sickly person didn't look like the healthy, good-looking athlete, with the boyish grin -- the man I'd learned to love unconditionally. Thank God his mind and spirit had not fallen victim to the cancer. Don's faith in our Lord had grown stronger, his relationship with Christ even closer, and our love -- well, it had become as polished gold, tested by fire. Don's mind was intact, while his ageless spirit, so vibrant and alive, awaited release and the fulfillment of Heaven. Again, I whispered through my tears, "I love you. Do you love me?"

Always before, he had answered, "Yes." However, the last few days, because of the heavy doses of morphine and other medication which made him sleepy, he had been barely able to answer.

He roused himself, and with all the strength he could muster, he moved his mouth, trying to say yes. Then he drew his last breath and died.

For a moment (or was it a lifetime?) I felt nothing and yet, at the same time, I felt everything. I experienced sadness, joy, loss, peace, relief, anger. My thoughts raced from here to there. How could Don be gone?

We had heard of people who, just prior to death, had experienced seeing deceased loved ones, a Brilliant Light, or some other manifestation of God's presence. Some had been able to share these moments with their loved ones, softening the impact of death. Apparently, this was not in God's plan for us.

I think I spoke aloud. "God," I said. "Please show Yourself in some way. Do something! Do it NOW!" I glanced toward the ceiling, hoping to see Don's spirit looking down at his body. I'd read about such things happening to people who had suffered a near-death experience. And who was more deserving than Don? Maybe he would still come back to me.

How long did I stand there waiting? I don't know if it was seconds or minutes, but it didn't matter because I didn't see anything. As tears of devastation and grief flowed from my eyes, I was forced to face the reality of the moment. "Okay, God," I finally said. "He's gone now and so is most of me. What are YOU going to do with the little bit of me that is left?"

How could I go on? Why had God led me to this moment? He, who gave me all my beginnings and endings, had allowed this to happen. If only Don and I could start over . . . If only I could once again be eighteen . . .

As I grew up, my main goal in life had been simply to marry a man who would love and take care of me, and allow me to take care of him. That was all I wanted -- that and raising a family. The dream was with me practically all the time, whether washing dishes or walking to and from school. My "knight in shining armor" would be very handsome, kind and gentle, with a sense of humor. He would be a hard worker and a good provider.

Well, I didn't find the "guy for me" in high school or business college -- the *knight* that every young girl dreams about. Still looking, I took a job with the Aluminum Company of America in New Kensington.

One afternoon, Loretta, a close friend, called and told me there was a dance at the Slovak Club. "Will you go with me?" she asked.

"Thanks for inviting me, but I think I'll pass."

"Come on," she coaxed. "You'll love the band -- they play great polkas! And there's this guy, Don, who will be there. He's a dental student at Pitt and plays basketball -- really good, too -- he's a star. Maybe we'll meet him!"

I'd seen Loretta with that dreamy-eyed look before. "Not again," I teased. "Aren't you ever going to learn that men are trouble. Me -- I'm through with them forever."

"Sure you are -- that is until you meet your knight."

"I'm beginning to think he doesn't exist." I had just broken up with a state police officer who wanted to marry me. He was a nice guy with a pleasant personality but I didn't love him. Besides, he wanted me to move in with his mom and dad after we got married. *Forget it,* I thought. *That's not what I want!*

"You have to stop brooding sometime," Loretta said.

"Oh, all right. But I'm going just to please you."

When Loretta picked me up at the house, she seemed excited about the evening. "We're going to have a great time; I just know it."

When we got to the club, we found a table near the dance floor.

"There he is," Loretta said enthusiastically. She was pointing to a tall, good-looking man who ambled toward our table. As he came closer, our eyes met and I sensed he was special. His contagious grin and honest expressive eyes seemed to sparkle with their approval of me. So much for my resolution about being through with men. Even before he spoke I was impressed.

"Hi," he said casually. "Want to dance?"

His voice melted away any reservations that I might have had. Without hesitation, I said, "I'd love to."

As we danced, I was delighted to discover that I had to look up to see into his face. At age eighteen, I was taller than most of the boys I had dated -- but that was not the case with this guy. I was to find out later that he was six feet, five inches tall. Right then and there, my heart told me I had found my knight. I'd heard about love at first sight and now I was experiencing it.

He wasn't much on small talk, so we just danced. Then he told me his name -- Don Virostek.

"You're so tall," I commented. "Are you a basketball player?"

"Yes, I play basketball. But let's talk about you -- what's your name?"

"Mary," I replied.

"The name doesn't fit you," he said. "With your dark hair and eyes, you look more like an Angeline."

Before the evening ended, we had danced every dance together and made plans to go to the club again the following week.

Shortly after arriving at the club for our first "official" date, it started to rain. Don suggested that, instead of staying there, we might go out and gather nightcrawlers.

"Nightcrawlers!"

"You know -- fishing worms. I'm going fishing tomorrow."

I was apprehensive. Looking down at my high heels, I said, "I'm not exactly dressed for the part."

"It'll be an adventure. Are you with me?"

The way he said it sounded like a challenge -- one I accepted.

The rain was falling lightly when we walked up a grassy hill near Don's home. He was armed with a

19

flashlight, a bucket and a can. And I soon learned to catch the four-inch worms that wriggled vigorously as though they knew the fate that awaited them.

"Hold the flashlight and the can," he ordered, his eyes searching the ground. "Aim it over here -- look, there's one!" He grabbed the worm before it could escape back into the ground. Don laughed in delight. "You're going to make a great meal for one big fish," he said.

"Yuk," I said, as we filled up the bucket with nightcrawlers. Most were king-sized and they left my hands coated with -- well, I don't know what it was but I didn't like it.

When Don took me home that night, a bit disheveled from my experience, he was pleased with the way the evening had gone. He had found a pal as well as a girlfriend. And me -- well, I knew I'd better start to like fishing worms and all that went with them because Don was definitely the outdoor type -- and I wanted to be *his* type.

2

I, MARY, TAKE THEE, DON . . .

I was born on Bryant Street in Vandergrift, Pennsylvania. The house Don built for me is only a block away from my childhood home. My life had been somewhat sheltered by my protective but loving parents. I could select my friends, but if they didn't agree with my choices, they would intervene. I did a lot of bike riding near my home, and in the winter I went sled riding and tobogganing with the other kids. Except for the state trooper, there had been no serious romance in my life. The few dates I had were innocent, usually double-dating with my twin sister, Josephine. She always wore skirts and makeup, while I was content to go out in jeans never bothering with makeup.

Don liked the natural side of me; he was unpretentious and truly tuned into nature. We got along extremely well, spending a lot of time at the river where Don would fish. We didn't talk because it would "scare the fish away." Don would bait his hook with a worm or a fly and cast for whatever fish would bite. I'd find a comfortable spot on a grassy bank and sit contentedly watching him fish. I would cook the fish that he had cleaned and prepared so expertly. They tasted delicious.

Our relationship deepened as we shared the quiet world of the river. The trees along the bank, the blue skies and breeze, the smell of frying fish, and the cozy campfires created an idyllic existence. There were no telephones or people to bother us. We tuned out the world and began to learn about one another. Soon *like* became *love, I* became *we,* and *my* future became *our* future. The world was wonderful and there was so much ahead for us.

We wanted a big wedding and a big wedding it was. On June 25, 1955, just ten days after Don graduated from dental school, we were married. For the first five months we lived in a cottage near Crooked Creek State Park at Ford City. A friend of Don's owned the cottage and let us use it without charge during the week. Weekends we returned home to avoid the intrusion of the crowds.

When Don graduated from dental school, I left my secretarial job at the Alcoa plant. Our only source of income was my unemployment compensation. It was a real blessing to have this rent-free, honeymoon cottage. This was a very special time for us and we made beautiful memories... Our days were filled with laughter, with having friends come to visit, cooking out, swimming and bathing by the dam. Not having running water and having to use an old hand pump to wash our dishes at the neighbor's, became a fun experience rather than a chore. We were living in a care-free world of love in the sunshine by the water. We had no worries -- just the freedom of being with each other in God's beautiful world.

In November 1955, Don enlisted in the Air Force as a Second Lieutenant. His goal was to gain experience in dentistry so when he was discharged, he could start his own practice. All of this came about just as planned.

At first I was homesick in Altus, Oklahoma, where the Air Force stationed us. I'd seldom been away from the home where I'd been born and raised. My father was a coal miner. He became involved in politics and spent a lot of time away from home, but we had a good relationship. Mom was loving but firm. I knew I could always count on her, no matter what!

I had grown up faithfully attending the local Catholic Church with Rose, Isabelle, and Josephine, my sisters, and my brother Sam. Even so, like many young people, I kept God at a comfortable distance in my life. He was rather like the close relative who lived in another state. I knew He was there, but we had very little communication. Maybe, If there had been communication, I would have been better able to handle my new responsibilities as a wife, and the adjustment to military life. I missed my family, my friends, and the security of familiar surroundings.

Not knowing anyone on the base made things worse. I didn't seem to fit in. I befriended the wife of an airman but this disturbed the Base Commander, who tactfully let me know what RHIP (Rank has its privileges) meant. Quite simply, I, as an officer's wife, was expected to fraternize only with my own class. Inwardly I rebelled, and the resentment grew.

Don and I both disliked socializing at the Officers' Club but were more or less required to spend some time there. The food was great but we intensely disliked the snobbery and meaningless chit-chat. Since we didn't drink, but had to appear to be sociable, we pretended to sip cocktails. Don and I didn't like these "games."

All my life I had been plagued with allergy problems, some of which affected my respiratory system. After moving to Oklahoma, the attacks worsened. I believed that my emotional state was contributing to the respiratory problems I was encountering, but was helpless in my ability to change things. The doctors at the base hospital kept me on sedatives which made me sleep a lot. Don became very concerned about my health and decided to take me to a clinic in Pittsburgh that specialized in respiratory ailments. He asked the Base Commander for permission to go. The commander didn't exactly deny Don's request but said he had a friend in Texas who was an excellent alleregist.

"That's closer than Pittsburgh," he said. "Why not take her there first, to see what he can do?"

We were granted an emergency leave and drove to Texas. After an examination and tests, the specialist said to me, "You have asthma and you're also allergic to practically everything except potatoes, ground beef and apples. You're so allergic you should be put in a garment bag and zipped up."

That began a twenty-year period during which I received several allergy shots each week. While the shots helped, I continued to suffer allergy attacks, usually at night. They terrified me and made me feel like I was suffocating. Each time I went through an allergic episode, my caring husband would bundle me up and take me for a ride. That and the sedatives helped me to sleep.

It was wonderful when Don was discharged and we returned to Vandergrift to begin a new phase of our lives -- a time when we would see our marriage bear much fruit. When I found out I was pregnant,

Don and I were thrilled beyond belief. But expectation was replaced by despair when we lost the child by miscarriage. Then on June 21, 1959, our first daughter, Judy was born -- a healthy, strong, beautiful baby. A year later I became pregnant again but also lost this child through miscarriage. We then were blessed with our son Andy, who was born on November 7, 1962. After another miscarriage, Tina came into the world on October 6, 1965, making her grand entrance right at home.

And so we were five!

3

GROWING TOGETHER

As a growing family, we spent most of our weekends at our camp in Kennerdell. At first it was a lot of work packing and unpacking diapers and bottles, and taking along what seemed like half of the house. But gradually, as the children grew older, I learned to enjoy it -- and I became a better packer.

Don and I continued to learn more about one another through living our daily lives as husband and wife. We became a reflection of one another in our ideals and goals, and yet, at the same time, we recognized and respected our differences as individuals. Sometimes these differences caused problems but, because our hearts were filled with love, our marriage stayed strong and fruitful.

Don was a quiet person, very much like his father. His mother was more of the "take charge" type of person. When we were first married, I had a problem getting a conversation going with Don. Even at work, his employees became frustrated when Don would choose to ignore a problem rather than face it. He especially hated to discipline people, even when they occasionally made mistakes.

There were times that I kept things from him, knowing he didn't want to be bothered by our day-to-day family problems. On other occasions, I would find myself getting annoyed by his silence and difficulty in sharing his intimate feelings with me. "Talk to me," I would say. "Tell me what's going on inside of you."

Don tried, but he just couldn't seem to communicate. I realized that he had never been really close to anyone in his life -- not even his parents. He had respect and love for both of them but, somehow, they never truly got to know one another. He and his dad had a friendly relationship but could not be considered as "friends." However, as Don grew as a Christian, he found many friends that he could count on for fellowship. And, of course, as his wife, I was his "best friend." This was very important to me and I took great joy in being able to give of myself to him.

I was definitely more outgoing than Don. Outward demonstrations of affection were natural for me, but not for him. He had a cool exterior and found it difficult to participate in such spontaneous behavior. Sometimes, it bothered me when he seemed to be so much in control of his emotions and actions. And, being a slightly stubborn person, I considered it a challenge when these situations occurred. Many of my seemingly impulsive actions were intentional efforts to make him a bit uncomfortable.

He was also reserved with our children -- refraining from spontaneously showering them with affection -- having trouble saying, "I love you." And yet they didn't seem to mind not receiving the outward demonstrations of his feelings; they *knew* he loved them.

Don delighted in Tina, our youngest daughter, who didn't hesitate to find ways to get his undivided attention. I remember with amusement the many times she would try to trick him when he came home from the office. He never knew what to expect. Sometimes she would lock the door, making him say "please," before letting him into the house. If Don didn't feel like saying please -- and he could be stubborn -- the real battle would start. Tina knew just how far she could push him before giving in and opening the door.

I remember a time when Tina was fifteen that she wanted to spend the night with a friend. The warning signals went up. I knew the mother wouldn't be home so I wanted to check out the situation to make sure Tina would be okay. However, Don didn't give me a chance. Without any discussion with me, Don airily dismissed the issue, saying, "Let her go; she's old enough." After Tina left for her friend's house, I let Don know how I felt about his carefree attitude.

"Something could happen to her," I pointed out. "Sure, I trust her -- but I don't trust the world."

Later on in life I learned that there are good reasons why I shouldn't trust the world. My complete trust should be in God!

When I called to check on Tina, I felt foolish about my concern since the girls were eating popcorn and having a great time.

Don was proud of Andy. It didn't take long for us to discover that he had an extraordinary ability in math. We were surprised to find that he could add and subtract before his fifth birthday. I had high hopes that Andy would follow in his father's footsteps as a dentist. I even told Andy that his dad might someday turn the dental practice over to him.

Andy, however, had no desire to become a dentist and nixed the offer. He had his own plans for life.

Our daughter Judy had a personality similar to her father's, so they occasionally had confrontations.

"You remind me of my mother," Don would say. "You're so sure of yourself."

"Just like you," she would quip back. "Neither one of us wants to back down when we think we're right."

In private Don would tell me how much he appreciated and respected her honesty. He felt that she was a level-headed person and he trusted her judgment.

When the children needed to be disciplined, Don tended to pull away. By default, I became the disciplinarian for the family, although I wasn't too great in this department. However, because our home was grounded in love, as well as an immature but growing faith in God, the children felt secure and never got into any serious trouble.

I enjoyed my very busy role as wife, mother and homemaker. I became a fulltime taxi driver, taking Judy to piano lessons, Andy to ball games, and Tina to and from school. My obligations changed and expanded as the children grew. Their road to independence caused us, as parents, to take pride in their achievements.

Don and I had an active social life, going out to dinner often, attending social functions, and becoming involved in church activities.

Don tried to be a handyman around the house, but that was not one of his strengths. My husband could can vegetables and cook, but when it came to fixing the plumbing, a frayed electrical connection, or a malfunctioning cabinet door, we called a repairman.

On weekends, when we weren't camping, Don kept busy with hunting, fishing and playing golf. His favorite season of the year was spring because he loved to see things grow. He spent many long hours working in his garden, planting vegetables, taking care of the tomatoes, onions, peppers, broccoli, carrots and the firm crisp lettuce that grows so well in the rich loam soil of western Pennsylvania. The corn and pumpkins he grew were the talk of the neighborhood. One year, we had a record-breaking pumpkin that weighed 250 pounds. There was even a write-up about it in our local newspaper.

Don could have been an excellent farmer if he hadn't chosen to become a dentist. Although he made a good living from his profession, there were many things about his work that he disliked. One of the problems was the large amount of stress involved in dentistry. Because of his gentle nature, it also bothered him whenever one of his patients experienced pain. He always went the extra mile to ensure their comfort. This man was so gentle that he would never even hurt a fly, unless it was tied to a fishing line, ready to go into the mouth of a large fish.

My husband showed his concern for others in many ways. For example, sometimes people would owe for dental work and have no money to pay for it. Of course, there were people who took advantage of this generous and caring attitude. Whenever this happened, what did he do? . . . He would write it off and make no attempt to collect the debt.

Although he had not yet fully tasted the "Living Water," he did have spiritual knowledge, and would try to show Christ's love and forgiveness through his actions. His witnessing was subtle -- he placed verses of Scripture and religious sayings on his office wall, where all who entered would see them. Don never initiated a conversation about religion, but if someone did, he would eagerly join in. God kept pulling Don closer to Him, and, at the same time, began using him to plant seeds of faith in others.

Yes, life was good for the Virosteks, but there would come a time for the testing of our faith. We would find ourselves reaching out for more of God and not being disapointed.

4

JESUS -- LORD OF OUR LIVES

"You know, Mary, we're having a good life, aren't we?"

"It's wonderful," I agreed. "It seems almost too good to be true."

Don and I were sitting on the couch. I was doing some cross-stitching; Don had his head on my shoulder. I paused to stroke his head.

He asked me, "Do you remember when we first got married and lived on your paycheck, rent-free in that cottage by the river? . . . And the fun we had swimming? . . . The corn roasts? . . . Boy, things were less complicated back then, weren't they?"

"They sure were. I will never forget those days."

"I even taught you how to swim."

"Taught me how to swim?" I playfully slapped at him. "You were a darn good swimmer, but you almost *drowned* me by having your friends tie that rope around my waist, and then telling me to jump off their shoulders."

Don said, "You weren't afraid of the water."

"That's different," I said. "It's one thing not to be scared of the water, and another thing to be thrown from somebody's shoulders with a rope tied around you."

Don grinned. "And I fished and caught a lot of big ones, didn't I?"

"You sure did. You were the best fisherman on the river."

He gave me a kiss. "That's because I had you with me. You can't do anything worthwhile without a partner, you know. And you're mine and always will be."

I felt something tug at my heart. It was one of those rare times when Don was being open with me, allowing his feelings to show. "It's been a great life," I said. "I hope it never changes."

But, of course, life does bring changes and sometimes pain. I remember a day when my world seemed to be shattered -- I came home from the doctor's office in tears after receiving some very devastating news . . .

"What's wrong?" Don asked.

"It's Mom! She -- she -- the doctor says she has cancer and only a few months to live." I gasped. "And she's only 59."

Don calmly picked up a glass of water from the table and took a drink.

I cried out, "What am I going to do without my mother? She's dying!"

Softly he said, "Everybody loses their mother, Mary."

For some reason that infuriated me. "I don't care about that," I said angrily, through my tears. "This is *my* mother we're talking about! She's always been there for me. When I was sick, she took care of me."

"And now you can be there for her. She's going to need you."

"But what can I do? She's dying."

"Let her know that you love her. Allow her to see your strength. Isn't that what she did for you?"

"Yes," I said, remembering how frightened I was when, as a nine year old, I was rushed to the hospital because I was bleeding internally. The bleeding was from the tonsillectomy I'd had in the doctor's office two weeks earlier. Clots had formed, and emergency surgery was required. Mom was in charge of all the decisions because my dad was out of town on political business. Her faith sustained her even though she was afraid of losing me. Having my mother there by my side gave me the courage to fight -- to believe everything was going to be all right. Her gentle hand in mine was the greatest medicine in the world.

Then, at age twelve, I had another brush with death. This time it was my appendix which had nearly perforated. During the three long weeks in the hospital, lying on my back, unable to turn over, I drew spiritual strength and learned patience from my parents. Their presence made me feel better; their words comforted me. And their love reassured me that I was surely going to get well. Mom told me that God's hand was upon me.

Don's voice interrupted my thoughts of the past.

"Mary, I love your mother -- you know that. Without her, I wouldn't have you." He continued somberly, "I trust in what she helped instill in you. You both have the same source of strength. God will help you."

Mom was suffering from cancer of the colon, and that had now spread to her liver. She was a short woman -- at one time rather heavy, but the illness had caused a drastic weight loss. Her name was

Virginia but everybody in the neighborhood called her Grandma Gina. She and my father, Sam, lived just down the street from us. They enjoyed a good life of traveling, seeing friends, and being real with one another. Mom would do the cooking and, afterwards, Dad would do the dishes. He was a happy man with a positive attitude. When speaking about death, one of his favorite sayings was, "Keep your suitcase packed, because when God is ready, He will take you. He knows where you live."

In the spring of 1974, my mother passed away. At that time, it was the worst experience of my life. But God, in His grace, had given me a person to help fill the empty place in my heart -- someone I could lean on. I'm talking about Don -- Jesus still didn't hold the proper place in my life.

My husband told me of a conversation with Mom which took place shortly before her death. "I'm not going to worry about Mary," she said to him matter-of-factly. "I know you will be there for her -- God will help you both."

Mom and I had gotten even closer while I cared for her, during her final days. I related to her symptoms. When she felt good, so did I. The same was true when she experienced pain or depression. When she thanked me for what I was doing, I shrugged it off by saying, "It's no big deal, Mom. I just want to do it for you."

Tears would well up in her eyes. "God will bless you for helping me, Mary. I'm sure your children will also be there for you when you need them."

"Mom, God has already blessed me. You know how bad my allergies have been -- well, a short time ago some of Don's staff members came over for lunch. While they were here, his dental hygienist suggested they pray for my allergies. I protested, saying that they should pray for others with more serious needs."

"So, what did they do?"

"They prayed for me, insisting that God could heal all things, no matter how large or small."

"Have you been healed?"

"Yes -- my doctor just confirmed that all my tests were negative. The allergies I've had for over 20 years are gone!"

"Mary, I'm so pleased for you, " she said weakly. "But my healing will come in Heaven and not here on earth . . ."

And then the morning came when she awoke in great pain -- she reached out and clutched my hand to her, barely able to say, "Mama loves you." The next day she slipped into a coma and died.

Her death changed my life. Up until that time, God and church were important to me, but other things had mattered more. No longer! At last, I truly committed my life to Christ, making Him the Lord of my life -- not simply accepting His saving grace. I finally began to realize His love was unconditional. What is this kind of love? To me it means that Jesus can love me, even when I don't agree with Him. I may not do or even say the things that He would want me to do or say, but it doesn't matter -- His love for me doesn't change. Recognizing that Jesus loves me unconditionally means that I don't have to do great things or perform in a particular way to win His favor. He loves me without placing requirements on my ability to perform. In return, I want to be the best that I can be -- showing my love by serving Him in every way that I can.

It felt strange to be without the person who gave birth to me and nourished me with loving care all of my life. Mom had been my best friend, and now she was gone. During her illness, I lost so much weight that I didn't have the strength to make it through the door of the funeral home -- Don had to help me.

Although I was drained physically, spiritually I was entering into a new realm.

God gave us Christian friends to help our family through this troubled time. We began to attend Bible study at a Presbyterian church -- there we dug deeply into the truths that are important to us. The Holy Spirit took over, giving us guidance as we grew in His word. After each meeting, we would go home and discuss the meaning of what we had just heard and learned.

Having made a commitment to Jesus, we continued to mature spiritually in our Christian walk. Our close friends had been praying for us, sensing what we were going through. One friend said to me, "Mary, nobody on this earth can help you with your hurt except Jesus."

I knew that what she said was true. Neither I, nor other people, could solve my problems; but God could and would if I only reached out to Him. I did exactly that -- and Don reached with me. We wanted more and more of Him.

Sister Bridget of St. Gertrude's Catholic Church, where we were members, spoke to me about my new enthusiasm. "You can be a blessing to our children, Mary. Why don't you teach for us?"

I had free time now, so I agreed to work with the eighth graders. It was a wonderful experience and I learned nearly as much as the children.

With our conversion experience, our personalities didn't undergo noticeable dramatic changes, but our hearts did. Jesus had said, "You must be born again," and we took Him at His word. We accepted the born-again experience and placed Christ in the center of our lives. We found that the intellectual acceptance of Jesus isn't enough. *Knowing* about Him just isn't the same as inviting Him to come and live inside of you, asking Him to fill you with the Holy Spirit.

Suddenly, I found that I had more compassion for others, especially those who didn't know the Lord. If I did something that was against God's plans, conviction would rise up inside of me. In a contrite spirit, I would then do everything possible to undo any damage resulting from my original action. Consciously, I would try to right the wrong. This was something I hadn't always done in the past. Now when I became angry, I realized in my heart that it was a sin. The Holy Spirit had me under such conviction in my spirit that I would have no other choice but to repent and say, "I'm sorry for being angry." *If a person is comfortable in sin, and there is no conviction, the battle is over. Satan has won!.*

Now if someone asks me, "How do you *know* you are saved? How do you *really know* you will go to Heaven if you die?" I can say, "I know that I know because of the conviction Christ has placed in my heart. I have repented of my sins, accepted what Jesus did at the cross for me, and now I am free." (2 Cor. 5:17 "Therefore if any man be in Christ, he is a new creature. Old things are passed away; behold, all things are become new.")

As our Christian experience deepened, Don and I found ourselves spending more and more time at our church. Once we were there, we never looked at the clock.

I love good sermons and become disappointed if a meeting takes place without the Word of God being spoken and discussed. Although Don wasn't a teacher, he eagerly sought to find Scriptures that were appropriate to our needs. He had always been a good listener but seldom made comments -- that is, until the time of our new commitment. He suddenly made a 180 degree change, wanting to talk and share his feelings. For the first time since we had met, he faced his shortcomings and fears head-on and and revealed them to others. I was so grateful to the Lord for giving him the courage, strength, and words to bring out these feelings.

He had always been close to our children, but now he grew even closer. He and Andy developed a special friendship, appreciating one another as individuals, not just as father and son. I thought, "God you are so wonderful and I'm so grateful for what you are doing for our family."

In 1983, I was taking care of my mother-in-law, who had suffered a stroke. From the moment we met, the two of us had a strained relationship because I believed I could never live up to her expectations. She wanted the "perfect" wife for her only son. I felt inadequate; it upset me to think that she might not totally accept me as a daughter-in-law. But Don said I shouldn't worry about it -- to just be myself. This turned out to be good advice because God had other plans for our relationship. During her illness we developed a close friendship as I ministered to her physically and spiritually. She also grew closer to her three grandchildren. At one point, she even acknowledged that Don had made a good choice for a wife. I knew this was an answer to prayer.

During this time, my father was diagnosed as having lung cancer. He had been smoking on a steady basis since he was twelve and the cigarettes had finally taken their deadly toll. When my mother-in-law improved sufficiently to move out, Dad then moved in. At first he was able to get around with the help of a cane, but, as his condition became worse, he was more and more dependent upon me for assistance. I prayed to God, asking Him to keep me healthy so that I would be able to take care of this man who had done so much for me. Several years later, when Dad went into a coma and died, the realization that both of my parents were now dead caused me to think more about my own mortality.

Life is so brief. It was now up to Don, my children and me to face the world without them. But I knew we weren't alone -- we had a wonderful, close friend. His name is Jesus!!

5

IN SICKNESS AND IN HEALTH

With stars in their eyes, and visions of a perfect life together, most couples repeat their wedding vows automatically -- not understanding that they are words of commitment and prophecy. Sickness, to some degree, will eventually invade a person's life and, when that happens, faith is tested, love is needed, and dependency, although difficult to accept, must be recognized. To a married couple, the words *"in sickness and in health,"* when put to the test, take on new meaning.

Through the years, Don and I began to understand the significance of *all* our wedding vows. We were closely bonded; oneness became a reality. When I felt pain, Don also hurt. When Don suffered, I felt his anguish. Spiritually, physically, and emotionally we were united.

I thank God that almost all of our years together were lived in good health. Yes, most of the time, life was good. Confidently, we faced the challenges of everyday living, secure because of our belief in God and in one another.

In 1983, something strange and frightening happened which caused me to start thinking more about my own health. It occurred on a holiday as we were entertaining members of our family and friends. It was a bit hectic for me -- dashing back and forth, making sure everybody was fed and had something refreshing to drink. Although I love to be around people, I found myself looking forward to having the party come to an end. After our company left, I walked into our den for a much-needed rest, feeling totally exhausted.

"Oh, Don, we had so much company," I said, yawning. I flopped into a chair and stretched out my legs. In an instant, I felt my strength leave me.

Don noticed the changed expression on my face.

"Mary, what's wrong?" he asked.

Trying to remain calm, I said, "Something -- something has happened to me."

I didn't know what it was -- I never had felt that way before. My arms and legs had become extremely weak.

Although Don was concerned, I made light of what was happening. "Don't worry, honey," I said, "I've just worked too hard."

Somehow, I regained enough strength to get up out of the chair and clean up the mess the others had made. I then went into the bedroom and laid on the bed. I telephoned a friend and mentioned to her what had happened. She said we should pray about it. We stayed on the phone for more than an hour, praying and sharing.

Even while I was talking to her, my left leg felt strange -- as if it didn't belong to me. I suppose I should have been afraid, but the power of prayer was already at work. After hanging up the phone, I fell asleep for several hours. When I awoke, I got out of bed and tried to turn on the light but couldn't lift my arm. I woke Don and started to say, "Honey, something terrible has happened to me!" I barely got the word *honey* out of my mouth when I collapsed to the floor.

He quickly came to me and helped me into the bathroom.

"Mary," he said grimly, "I'm taking you to the hospital."

I protested, but without much conviction in my voice. I didn't know what was happening to me, but I continued to pray, turning it over to the Lord. "God this is in your hands," I said with assurance as we drove toward the hospital.

After reviewing my medical tests, the doctors felt that there was a possibility of a brain tumor. When Don heard this, he came over to me and asked. "Mary, what is the worst thing that could happen to you?"

"I could die," I replied.

He did not hesitate with his response. "If that happened, I would have the problem -- not you. You would be gone but I would be left behind."

Additional tests did not confirm the tumor diagnosis, and the doctors decided I was suffering from a severe case of exhaustion. My strength quickly returned. How I praise God for hearing our prayers and intervening in this situation! The Bible says we are fearfully and wonderfully made, and I believe it. All of our faculties work together to give us pleasure: arms, legs, heart, mind, senses. I greatly sympathize with anyone who has lost the use of a limb or any of the senses. For a brief moment I was there and, you have my word, it is not an experience I would care to repeat. It did, however, give me some insight into Don's feelings when, later on, I saw his frustration and helplessness as his body betrayed him.

"Mary, my back hurts. It's really hurting. Maybe we'd better go home."

It was a cool night in March 1986. Spring was just around the corner. We were visiting friends and Don was in pain. His back had been hurting him for some time. We both thought it might be attributed to his sitting in one position for such a great deal of his time at work. That must be what was wrong with him! No big deal!

Don's physician had previously prescribed muscle relaxants and pain pills for his back problem. At first these helped, but eventually they didn't have any lasting effect in easing his discomfort.

"You'd better go back to the doctor," I suggested.

Don shook his head. "It's just a muscle spasm. It'll go away."

However, it didn't go away; it only got worse.

Because of this, we left our friend's house early and, on the way home, I again told him he should see a doctor. The more I insisted, the more he procrastinated saying, "I can't leave my patients -- they need me!"

Four months passed. Finally on July 4, the pain became so intense that he couldn't walk. That was enough for me! I took charge and told him, like it or not he **WAS** going to the hospital.

Don literally had to be carried from our home to the ambulance for the trip to West Penn Hospital. Even in this condition, he still tried to minimize our fears. When we arrived, the emergency room physician took care of him since our family physician was not available. Radiological tests were ordered but the X-rays came back showing no abnormalities. Don was given medications and told to come back for further evaluation by a specialist.

On Monday when we returned, the neurosurgeon thought that Don probably had a slipped disc or possibly a tumor. He told us he was admitting him for further testing.

"Tumor?" The word sent shock waves through me. Don couldn't possibly have a tumor -- he was too healthy. I began praying for my husband as they prepared to take him to his room.

Sam, my brother, who worked at the hospital came to Don's room to see us. "Don't worry," he said. "Everything will be fine. I'll be back to see you tomorrow."

Later that day Sam and the doctor came back to the room. As soon as I saw my brother's face, I knew something was wrong. His eyes were avoiding mine. Inwardly, I felt apprehensive -- the news would not be good. The results were in!

The doctor walked over to the foot of Don's bed. Reaching down he took hold of Don's feet and soberly spoke, "Before I explain our findings, I want you to know that you are going to need your faith, family and friends to make it through this." He paused, then, looking up at Don, continued speaking. "You have a malignant tumor wrapped around your spine."

Don paused for a moment, then said, "That's okay. I win either way. Either I will get well or I will die and be with the Lord." He then quoted from Psalm 116:15, "His loved ones are very precious to Him and He does not lightly let them die."

At the doctor's words, my mind went into shock -- rejecting what I had heard. I couldn't understand Don saying that it didn't matter if he lived or died.

The reality of the situation was too much for me. It must have shown on my face because my brother came over and said, "Let's go out in the hall and talk."

I didn't protest as he took my arm and ushered me out the door. Shortly afterward, we were joined by the doctor who wanted to know if I had any questions. I had many questions I wanted to ask but couldn't because my mind was numb from shock.

In my confusion I said, "I don't even know what to ask you."

"That's all right; you don't have to ask anything now. If you should think of something later I'll be here for you." He then continued, "I'm ninety-nine percent sure it is prostatic cancer. We have two options: we can do a bone marrow or an actual surgical biopsy."

Several key words that the doctor had spoken echoed over and over again in my mind, magnified in sound as if I were hearing them over a loudspeaker. *Cancer ... Bone marrow ... Surgery ... Biopsy ... Ninety-nine percent sure.* Then I remembered what he had said to Don about faith, family and friends to get through it all. It was the word *faith* that my mind finally locked into -- faith in an awesome God who has infinite power! He could heal Don instantly or He could do it through the doctors. I reassured myself that Scripture says nothing is impossible for Him. All we have to do is ask -- and wait in faith. God understood how much I needed Don; it just had to be in His will to intervene -- to stop Satan in his tracks.

My husband was my life; I'd always drawn from his courage and strength. When we lost our babies -- when our parents died -- when I was sick -- he had been there. "God," I cried, "I'll trust You, even though I don't like this intrusion."

Having no control over a situation frightened me; I hated the unknown. I wanted things to stay the same. Life with its joys and blessings was wonderful but I didn't like the curves.

I used to ride my bicycle around the neighborhood, feeling the wind on my face as I cruised down hills and went around corners. How I loved the sense of freedom, the feeling of control! However, when I came close to wrecking, or felt a hint of danger, I became apprehensive. Was the ride worth it?

It was the same thing when my friends and I went sled riding during the snowy winter months. The rides weren't dangerous unless someone ran into a snow covered tree trunk or rock. Most of the kids enjoyed this element of danger -- but me -- well, I wanted the sled ride but not the risk.

"Oh, God," I said aloud. "Why are there curves in life? ... Why are there times we lose control? ... Why are there tree trunks or rocks along the way? ... Why did You allow this to happen to us? ... Haven't we been good people? Aren't we raising a good family dedicated to moral principles, to loving and serving You? We're Christians -- not only in name, but in practice."

When Don's surgery was done, it confirmed the diagnosis of prostate cancer. It also, temporarily, reduced some of his pain and several days later Don was discharged from the hospital.

Don accepted the findings with a positive attitude. I didn't! He wasn't concerned with the "why," but simply believed God would heal him. His faith was incredibly strong and also contagious. After the initial shock wore off, I not only spoke faith, but began to live it. Don *would* be healed and we could then go on with our lives as before. When he retired from dental practice, we would be together all the time. It would be just the two of us, loving each other, doing things for one another, going on his beloved fishing trips, and sitting in the shade of a tree in the summer while the river rolled by. How wonderful it would be, venturing to the edge of eternity, excitedly contemplating our love and lives in the now, and yet realizing that *this was not the end of it!* There would be greater things in store for those who loved the Lord!

When my friends learned Don had cancer, they went out of their way to be kind. Many people of all faiths approached me and asked what they could do. Some prayed. All expressed their friendship and love. Vandergrift, our hometown, was responding in a positive way to our crisis.

Right from the beginning, Don fought hard for his life. He continued to fight as he later went through radiation and chemotherapy treatments, periods of hospitalization, and stays at a rehabilitation center.

Shortly after Don's diagnosis was made, we were able to go to Virginia Beach for a week. For the past several years we had gone with Don and Jeannie and, somehow, now it seemed crucial for us to go ahead with our plans. It was an attempt at normalcy. Even though there was heaviness in our hearts, it turned out to be a very special week of sharing. Every moment together seemed so precious... We concentrated on the present, not the future. We thought about the past and where our marriage had taken us...

When two people choose to live in the holy sanctity of marriage, they are strangers, setting off on an unknown journey. Don and I had been strangers, despite our attraction toward each other-- an attraction that grew into love. Our relationship was certainly not perfect at the start. What relationship is? But we chose to work on it. To me it was like a puzzle that had to be solved and I was willing to do everything in my power to piece it together.

Raising children together had been such a beautiful experience. And now, with two of them married, our family was expanding.

Judy attended Bradford Secretarial School and then went to Duquesne University for a year. In 1980 when she married Pete, we were pleased. He and Don became very close friends. Their daughter, Nicole, brought new life and excitement into our lives. We were typical grandparents, doing our share of bragging and showing photos. Nicole spent as much time as possible with *"Pap Pap."* He took her to the garden to pick strawberries and put them on her cereal -- a real treat for her. He taught her to garden and spent many hours on his knees with her in the soft rich dirt, digging up weeds and helping her to develop a "green thumb." When Nicole realized her Pap Pap was sick, she would place her little hand on his knee, close her eyes and ask Jesus to, *"Please heal my Pap Pap."* Blessed? Yes, indeed, dear Lord.

Andy, a successful businessman, had married Suzanne, a beautiful girl who was a real joy and blessing to Don and me. She was an "up" person and a delight to be around -- a pleasant addition to our family.

Then I thought about Tina who had attended Penn State for a year and, afterward, enrolled at Geneva College. As a competent accountant, she was working toward her CPA.

Our children had witnessed God's love at work in their parent's lives -- a love that had been growing over the years, and now was even stronger as we struggled against the cancer. We were eagerly reaching toward the perfection level that God asks that we try to attain. Now that cancer had interrupted our lives, *"in sickness and health,"* had become a reality.

We both thanked the Lord for bringing us as far as He had in our spiritual lives. I knew that many married couples never achieved the level we had reached, so we were especially blessed. But, oh, how I wanted the opportunity to continue to grow in this love -- to practice it further -- to live it in the way our Creator intended.

6

COMMUNITY OF ANGELS

Following a series of radiation treatments as an outpatient, Don was readmitted to West Penn Hospital on September 10, 1987. He was unable to even lift his head. X-rays indicated that the tumor on his spine had grown so large that it was threatening to cause a compression of his spinal cord. The doctor told us there were two options available: radiation therapy or surgery. Don asked what he should do, and then left the decision up to the doctor. It was decided that surgery would be the best option -- it was scheduled for the following Monday. That weekend I prayed and contacted many friends, asking them to also pray about this decision.

On Sunday night, the doctor, returning from a weekend trip, came to Don's room. He told him that earlier that day, while he was in church, Don came into his mind. He prayed about their decision and now felt that immediate surgery was not imperative. He first wanted to see how Don would do wearing a special brace. God heard our prayers, those of the doctor and our friends; Don was spared the pain of surgery.

During the next five months, he was transferred three times to the Harmarville Rehabilitation Center. The staff was efficient and well trained, showing compassion and concern for our physical and emotional needs. After a few weeks, however, he would have to return to the hospital for more intensive treatment. For the final three months of his life, there were no further transfers to Harmarville. West Penn Hospital became our home away from home.

While Don was bedridden, just as *any* wife would do, I did all I could to make his days more comfortable. He noticed this and would often look at me with loving eyes of gratitude.

"Mary, when this is over and I get out of here, I'm going to treat you extra special for a whole year -- just because you are *you*."

"Shush," I said. "Just get well and that will be my reward."

For the first time in my life, I realized that material things aren't important; relationships are! Property, a beautiful home, cars, a bank account -- none of these things mattered unless I could share them with the man I loved. As long as God was in our hearts -- and we had each other -- we had it all.

I became more concerned; my fears began to intensify. ***Why wasn't he getting any better?***

Don's primary physician was a man who talked sparingly, yet he answered our questions patiently and in full detail. And we had many questions for him about cancer, Don's condition, his prognosis, and what, if anything, I could do to help. He was a quiet, sympathetic man who readily showed his concern for both of us. In response to Don's suffering, his favorite expression was, "We'll explore the pain." Then he would prescribe the appropriate pain medication. Surely, God has blessed this man with unique gifts which will continue to ease the suffering of other patients.

Another doctor, who was on the oncology team, was a lover of sports. Naturally, he and Don talked a lot about football, basketball, and baseball. Their rapport grew as they chatted with enthusiasm about various players and the potential and performance of certain teams. It was all Greek to me -- what did I know about sports? But they got along famously.

When Don and I were first married, we would, on occasion, go to see the Pittsburgh Pirates or the Steelers play; but I didn't really get into sports until our son began to play basketball. That fanned my interest in basketball a little and became the extent of my sports' knowledge. I suppose quite a few people would be surprised by my ignorance when one considers Don's lifetime passion for sports. Under the legendary Vandergrift High School coach, Oscar J. Schneider, Don played both baseball and basketball. Later, after he was admitted to the University of Pittsburgh Dental School, he won the Athletic Committee Award for his four outstanding years of basketball at Pitt. With each season playing center for the Pitt Panthers, his ability improved. He placed fifth in the nation in rebounds. Not bad for a kid from East Vandergrift!

As Don's treatment continued, I came to realize that the hospital was a lot like the community where I had grown up -- everybody had a function and a reason for being there. Here in this beehive of activity was a community of medical experts and technicians, each steeped in his or her own specialty, coming to grips with whatever disease crossed their path. There was no magical formula or set cure. Each patient required his or her own special treatment, and the hospital team responded with all the expertise at their command.

I marveled at their efficiency even as fear swept over me that perhaps they could not do enough to offset the cancer that was destroying my husband. Then something would happen: a brief alleviation of pain, an X-ray, or encouraging lab report -- and my hopes would rise again. It was comparable to being on a roller coaster. One moment you are way down in the valley; the next moment, you're hurtling toward the crest at a dizzying rate of speed. My emotions were not geared to this, but I had no choice but to accept it. And I knew -- knew down deep in my soul -- that I must never discourage Don. I would try to control my ups and downs, projecting my belief in the doctors' ability to cure him with God's help. That was my pledge to myself; that was my prayer. I couldn't dampen Don's optimism with my frustration that he wasn't getting any better.

A close friend, Billy, who was a healing evangelist from the Pittsburgh area, would frequently visit Don and me in the hospital to pray. Privately he told me that we should go along with Don and not discourage him. One Friday we prayed that God would give my husband the strength to accept whatever God's will would be for him.

Three days later, on Monday, Don looked at me and said, "What if I'm not healed?" This was the first indication that he realized that his healing might not take place on this earth.

As the days passed, the hospital became my world. Outside the confines of this medical establishment, the joys and struggles of life went on, but I was oblivious to their existence.

Since Don was too sick to leave his room, my day consisted of routine procedures such as taking the steps down to the first floor where the cafeteria was located. Perhaps I'd buy a daily paper or even stop at the gift shop. At some point, I found myself automatically counting the number of steps I had to descend to get to my destination. There were thirty-three. Of course, then it was back up the thirty-three to return to the room. I also discovered that it was exactly thirty-five steps from Don's room to the nursing station. The counting and walking gave me both physical and mental exercise. I was used to walking at least two miles a day prior to Don's illness so I reasoned that the more trips I made, the better it would be for my health. Going out of the room took me away from Don but returning always gave me a feeling of joy and hope. He was there for me -- he was waiting for me.

"Oh, God," I'd pray. "Keep him alive, and give me the strength to be here for him."

I was so busy being with Don that I neglected my appearance. I usually slept, fully dressed in "sweats," on a cot by Don's hospital bed. Some days I didn't even take time to bathe or change clothes. I knew my hair needed to be cut and colored -- but it just wasn't possible.

"That's okay, God," I'd say. *It's just for a season."*

Don had never been the type to give compliments, so I was touched when he told me ot a conversation he had with our daughter Tina.

"You know," he said, "your mom is very special and should be woman of the year."

I laughed when I heard this since I was quite aware of my shabby, unkempt, and scruffy appearance. Our love was truly becoming unconditional. I knew Don wasn't looking at my appearance or remembering my civic contributions or achievements -- he was looking at my heart. He saw Jesus in me. This just reaffirms that it is not us, but Christ in us, who makes us someone special!

As I continued to go up and down the hospital steps and to walk around the hospital proper, I discovered that the faces of the staff had become more than just faces. These were people who cared; they were friends. In a way, they were family. This is where I was living -- where Don was fighting for his life.

One day when I couldn't control my frustration and pain, I broke into tears. Joyce, one of the nurses, placed her arms around me.

"Hey, it's okay to cry, Mary," she said soothingly. "After all, God made tears, too."

Kathy, another nurse, also showed great understanding, and talked with me about trusting in God. "He knows how you feel." she said. "He loves you."

Kathy and Sarah, the two clerks in the 3-C Section, always had time for me. When Don was receiving his series of radiation treatments, we would frequently talk.

"Mary, do you need something from the cafeteria?" Kathy would ask. They would go there for me and get a glass of tea or a cup of coffee. And they really loved Don. Anything he would ask for, they would get for him -- no matter what time of day or night it was.

Then there was Sue. She came in one day while Don was undergoing radiation therapy, and said, "Let's walk through the park." She added, "If you want to talk, I'll listen."

Talk about a friend! She seemed to know exactly what to say, how to say it, and when to leave me in silence.

I remember one day when I went to the cafeteria to get my dinner -- it turned into a total disaster! The kitchen crew had made beef stroganoff in gravy, poured over rice. I carried it out on my tray and walked into Don's room.

He scowled, saying sharply, "I can't bear the smell of that food."

His reaction and the tone of his voice surprised me, but I managed to control myself. When he asked me to take the tray outside the room and eat, I told him that that would be fine with me.

However, as I picked up the tray to leave the room, it slipped out of my hands -- the gravy, rice and beef splattered all over the floor.

I looked at the mess in stunned silence and a flood of tears rolled down my cheeks. I couldn't stop crying. Sue heard the disturbance and hurried into the room. She looked at Don and at me and, without a word, began to clean up the mess. I helped her, sniffing miserably. Don just lay there in silence.

Finally, he said in a more gentle tone, "Mary, why are you crying?"

Why am I crying? I wanted to explode. I stuttered and stammered, trying to make him understand about the food, my emotions, his condition -- but the proper words wouldn't come out.

"Mary," he said kindly, "go to the cafeteria and get yourself the best sandwich they make."

"No," I said stubbornly as I left the room. "I'm not hungry." And I wasn't and I didn't.

After pacing the hallway for a few minutes to calm down and get my thoughts in order, I returned to the room and sat down in a chair next to Don's bed. Taking his hand in mine, I smiled and apologized. We then prayed together for forgiveness.

There were times when Don's veins were hard to reach with IV needles. As they probed, trying to find a vein, I would pray silently. "Please God, help them to find a vein. Don't let them hurt him." And it seemed that my prayers were always answered as they quickly and painlessly did their job.

One day, Don was experiencing great pain. The drugs didn't seem to be working, and changing his position didn't help either. I was feeling frustrated and near tears when the nurse walked in. She found that the source of his excruciating pain was caused by a clogged catheter.

"I'll take care of that," she said firmly.

She changed it and the pain left almost immediately. I know this is just a routine incident, and is what is expected from the nursing staff in a hospital, but I was so grateful to her. Any relief from pain was a victory for us. "Thank you, Jesus," I said from my heart.

We had been up most of that night, and both Don and I were exhausted. Sue, sizing up the situation, closed the door and said, "We're all done now and nobody is going to bother you. Get some sleep." And she was gone.

We quickly fell asleep and slept soundly for several hours. When Don awoke, he called Sue and said, "Give me a hug. Thanks for taking care of my problem."

Sue was not an unusual example of the exemplary care provided by the entire nursing staff. They were all excellent caretakers. It helped to know that others understood what I was experiencing emotionally. It had reached the point where I could no longer deny the physical evidence of Don's deteriorating condition.

Pastor Phil, the hospital chaplain, in his quiet caring way, helped me to come to grips with the obvious fact that Don was not getting any better. Our conversations helped prepare me for the eventuality of Don's death. Later, after Don's death, he also helped me through the grieving process. He is truly a chosen vessel -- a man of God.

Of course, just as families sometimes have problems -- there were also difficult moments with some members of the staff. Don's pain had progressed to the point where he required continual morphine to handle it. And he also needed other medications intravenously every six hours to enhance the pain-killing effects of the morphine. One day, when Don was in a lot of pain, I went to find a nurse. They were all busy with other patients and could not respond to his needs as quickly as we would have liked. When you are hurting, a minute seems like forever.

When the nurse arrived, a few moments later, I was on my cot, crying. At this point, tears were my only outlet for my inward emotions of anger and frustration. I spoke rather harshly. "Where have you been? What took you so long? I can't stand to see my husband suffer!"

She was taken aback by my obvious agitation and said, "I'm sorry I didn't get here as soon as you would have liked, but I have other patients to take care of. Maybe you should consider hiring a private duty nurse for your husband."

Before I could give the curt reply that was on the tip of my tongue, Don intervened.

"Forgive us," he said to the nurse. "We are hurting."

She then left the room.

I prayed quietly to the Lord: "God, I am asking you to forgive me for my temper. How can I possibly ask for a miracle when I have anger in my heart toward others.

When the nurse returned, I asked her forgiveness. She looked startled -- and then we hugged. At that moment, I knew we could become friends for life.

7

A LETTER TO JESUS

I had never really understood how terrible the torment of pain could be until Don became ill. Pain is reality, like a mountain or a desert, or a tall tree standing in your back yard. It is not a figment of one's imagination. It is there -- and it can be a killer.

It staggered my imagination to see the immense quantities of drugs the doctors administered to my husband to relieve him of his suffering. And yet they were all necessary so that Don could function as a human being for as long as possible. I didn't want them. He didn't want them. But he *NEEDED* them. And so it was done.

As the disease continued its journey, the pain killers were administered to him in heavier doses. Cancer is more than pain; it robs the body of its ability to take food. Don, who normally had a hearty appetite, lost his zeal for eating. He drank four ounces of apple juice, six ounces of beef broth, chicken broth, gingerale or water. Sometimes the dietician would vary it -- apricot juice or milk, or a soft drink.

Drugs and juices. Juices and drugs. And all the while my husband's body wasted away, consumed by the ravaging effects of the destroyer within him. One day, in anguish and desperation, I wrote a letter to our Lord.

Dear Jesus:

I love you, I thank you for dying to save us, to heal us, and to give us eternal life.

I don't understand how the enemy has gotten the power over us and is destroying Don's body with his wicked hand. I just don't understand; I don't understand at all.

Tell me, Lord Jesus, why haven't you healed him? He has believed so strongly that he was going to be made whole. Why?

We love you, Jesus. We thank you for loving us more than we could ever love. Please, Lord Jesus, let me know why. Is there something we cannot see as yet? I know you are a fair God -- but do you really care? When you bled and died on the Cross, your suffering gave us the victory and power over Satan. Help us to understand what is now happening in our lives. Please answer as soon as you can because I need to be set free from what I feel is the work of the Evil One. We love you lots! Thank you Jesus.

Love,

Mary

P.S. Jesus, I hurt badly; Don hurts badly. There is so much pain, so many tears. Please give us peace!

This letter of prayer expressed the way I felt deep down inside. Tearfully, I read the letter to Don, who smiled but made no comment. The words helped me to feel closer to God. But, would they help Don? Spiritually, he remained strong; but slowly and surely, he was being burned out -- emotionally and physically.

Because of the effects of the medication, Don would alternate between periods of extreme sleepiness and rational awareness. One time, toward the end, Don struggled to make conversation. "Mary," he began, in a voice surprisingly strong, "I want you to remarry."

"Wha -- What?"

"I said, I want you to remarry. I mean it."

"Don, I'm married to you. I always will be!"

But, he was determined to pursue the subject. "Mary, if we have to say goodbye, it would be best for you to get married again. I can't stand the thought of you being alone."

"Don, didn't you hear what I said? I don't want -- "

He continued on, ignoring my protests. "It won't be disrespectful -- just remember, though, that I'll be waiting in Heaven for you."

I started to cry. "I feel like you are rejecting me."

"That's not true! It's because I love you that I'm thinking about your future."

Even though I knew why he was saying these things -- that it was the result of our "unconditional love," I didn't want a future without him.

I prayed again and again, asking God to make our lives normal. I wanted things the way they had been before. "Please, Lord," I begged. "I will serve you all the days and years of my life if you will grant me this one prayer."

Being bold was easy. We knew Jesus had promised to keep us in His care. Each evening, I would read the Scriptures to Don, going over his favorite verses, and finding others that seemed appropriate to the moment and to what was happening in our lives. And Don would listen, nod, and finally fall into an untroubled sleep. Oh, what bliss came over his face! The ravages of that deadly cancer could not destroy the peace he felt in his soul!

We lived on faith -- something the doctors said we would need. It was a blessing to hear these men admit that all their skills, chemicals, and surgical procedures could not replace the simple act of faith. Faith is still the heart's final hope. Faith is still a gift of God.

Faith carried Don through the most difficult times. Even as he lay suffering, his faith would shine through in remarkable ways. It carried over to those around him -- the hospital staff, our family and friends, priests and pastors. Some of these people were strangers, who in turn shared his example of faith with others.

Don and I wanted to make a statement -- for all to see -- that we believed strongly in God and His love for us despite the apparent circumstances. By playing our Christian tapes, openly displaying our Bibles, and praying together, we were able to witness for Christ. This was our way of telling others of the peace and joy He provided, even in our darkest moments.

8

THE TRAIN TO HEAVEN

I began experiencing anger toward God. Scripture was becoming more meaningful to Don, but I was still puzzling over unanswered questions. Why wasn't the Word being manifested to us? Nothing was making sense. How could Don keep believing when it did not appear that anything was happening? Things were going from bad to worse.

Once, while in prayer, I sensed that God was telling me that Don would be made whole in His Kingdom. I rejected this with my whole being.

Oh no! Lord, I thought, *please don't take him yet. I need him. Oh, how I need him!*

Don looked at me as though he knew what I was thinking. "Mary," he said, "Dying isn't so hard. It's leaving you that's going to be difficult. But we have to face reality."

As the grim threat of death hovered over him, I was forced to acknowledge that time was running out for us. Why were we so powerless? At times I felt depressed, wanting to give up.

Once, while resting on the hospital cot, I heard the fire whistle sound. It was very late and I knew this could not be a practice drill. Someone came and closed our door -- a part of the procedure which they always followed in the event of a fire. Don's room was located at the end of the hallway and, because he couldn't move about, I was sure that we were trapped. I knew that I'd never leave his side -- not even if it meant dying in a fire with him. In a way, it was an escape for me, a way which would allow us to go on into eternity together. Since, in my heart, I felt as if I were already dying with him, what did it matter?

In a few moments, I looked out the window and saw the fire trucks leaving; then the fire whistle blew again, telling everyone that the danger had passed. The fire was out! God had protected us. Was I relieved? . . . I'm not sure.

I continued to wait for a reprieve from God -- to see Don suddenly and miraculously get up and out of that hospital bed. "Dear God," I'd plead, "don't let this happen to Don -- to us. We're your trusted servants."

The nurses realized long before I did that I didn't want to let go of my husband -- to release him to God. They knew that he wasn't going to make it, and that there was nothing medical science could do to keep death from taking its toll. They tried to make me face the reality of the situation. Several even encouraged me to talk about death, but I just couldn't do it. My silence was a protest, a way of hiding inwardly from something my mind couldn't comprehend. Never would I accept it -- it would be showing a lack of faith. Regardless of how things looked, Don would not die! I would will him to live; God *would* do His miracle!

Don continued his counseling efforts in my behalf. "Mary, what do you think about death?"

This time, I allowed the door to open, just a little. "I don't know. What do you think about it?"

He said thoughtfully, "I guess I'm willing to get on the *'train'* to Heaven and be with the Lord."

"You may be," I said, with an edge to my voice. "But what about how I feel?"

"Mary, I know you hurt. I can feel it. But, through this experience -- the fear, anger, and horrible pain, I've found out what faith is really all about. I can say, *'That's okay, God; I'll trust You.'*"

"But I can't give up. I can't give *you* up."

"You have to accept God's will and then get on with your life. I have been praying and know that you will have a ministry working with people, perhaps widows."

Don could sense my doubts so he asked me to read Ephesians 3:20 from his Bible. "Now glory be to God who by His mighty power at work within us is able to do far more than we would ever dare to ask or even dream of -- infinitely beyond our highest prayers, desires, thoughts, or hopes."

"Don, please -- let's talk about something else," I said, feeling uncomfortable talking about life without him in it.

But he wasn't going to be put off. "Mary, there are things that have to be decided. I think you should keep the house." He paused, then continued thoughtfully, "I wouldn't sell the jeep since it will be a good vehicle to get you through the winter months."

I didn't respond to any of his comments or suggestions, convinced that to do so would show my lack of faith. I was dependent on my husband and proud of it. Don was my world and I wanted to keep him.

One afternoon I was really tired, but couldn't rest because Don was having a really bad day. A student nurse told me to try to sleep. "I'll watch over him," she said. "Lay down on the cot!" I took her advice and instantly fell asleep.

When I awoke, Carol, the nursing instructor, was there. She motioned to the door. "I want to see you outside," she said.

Puzzled, I followed her to the hallway. "Okay, what is it?" I said. She seemed anxious -- upset.

"I want to talk to you about Don." She hesitated, then began again. "You know, he wants you to release him. He told the student nurse that he was on the train, ready to leave, but that you won't let him go."

"I can't," I gasped. "I just can't."

"Yes, you can," she argued. "He's suffering and is waiting for your permission to die." Her voice softened. "Please, tell him that it's okay."

Her words convicted me of my selfishness. My eyes met hers. "Not yet -- but soon."

Days passed. I was alone with Don, looking at his gaunt face, feeling the pain he was going through. I sobbed, calling on the name of God. "You're going to take him, aren't you? Okay," I said, finally, feeling numb. "I guess I have to say,'*That's okay, God,*' but I have no peace."

Then I whispered words of release to Don. "Honey, I know you're on the train -- when it's time, go ahead and leave." These words spoken to Don were the beginning of my own healing process.

Immediately, my mind challenged my words. *Oh, Lord, what have I done?*

Don looked relieved, almost happy. I knew our Lord would soon be coming to claim his soul.

How I wanted to believe -- truly believe in my heart that it was really okay for Don to go. Could I live with what I had said? Satan caused a battle to rage within me. Don would be gone and I would be all alone. How could I handle that? For five months -- five long months, I had lived by his side, sleeping in the room with him, while he labored for breath. I watched him try to eat as he fought the cancer that was robbing his body of its vitality.

Did I regret the time spent there? . . . Not a moment . . . I would have stayed there forever. I didn't realize what strength I had in me until it was needed for my husband.

Before and during Don's hospitalization, God blessed us with many people who were always there to help whenever there was a need. The blessings brought by these friends manifested themselves in many different ways, according to our needs. There were some people who came to visit regularly to pray and offer encouragement. Judy and Dave Nelson are an example. In fact, they literally gave up two years of their social life for us. Others told how they fasted and prayed at home, feeling God's comforting presence surrounding our situation. One couple came to visit, ministering through words and music. Their soothing songs would momentarily cut through any depression we might be feeling.

Then there were those who offered practical help such as going grocery shopping, running errands, and doing laundry. Tony, my brother-in-law, would offer to cut the grass and stay with Don so that I could get away from home for awhile. Many times, when I felt too exhausted to cook, there would be a knock at the door and someone would be there with food. Even one of Don's patients, a man with multiple sclerosis, stopped by to see him and offered encouragement and inspiration. The dentist who worked with Don, and the entire office staff were a tremendous blessing. They kept things running smoothly. Flo, the office dental assistant, made daily visits to bring him the office mail. These visits were reassuring to Don and helped keep him busy and interested in his work.

Don had thought he would make it because of his faith . . . and because of the support and love of people. How wonderful that God never leaves us in our time of need! He provides friends, relatives, and even the natural elements of the earth to give us all we need to get through a personal crisis. Although Don was losing the battle, he had the ultimate victory because the threat of death was no longer frightening to him. He was looking forward to Heaven, and to spending eternity with Jesus.

But me, I still clung to the hope that God would intervene -- even as I could see the disease eating deeper and deeper into his body. As the pain and discomfort increased, Don's faith actually grew stronger. There was no stopping him. He had turned his face to the Son and would continue his journey onward and upward, a triumphant march on into eternity.

I wanted to be strong too; but often I lashed out at God. "Heal him!" I demanded. "Heal him right now! Haven't we done everything that is required of us? Our faith is whole; our minds and hearts are fixed on you. What more can we do, Lord, to please you and to receive what you have promised in your Word?"

"Where is He?" I asked Don. "Where is this God you are trusting in?"

"Mary, He *is* here. Don't you doubt it for a moment."

He had reached the point where he was trying to comfort me. I was supposed to be the comforter but, instead, my dying husband was telling me to have faith. "Everything will work out. God is in charge," he would say reassuringly.

Jesus spoke to the storm. "Quiet down," He commanded. The wind and waves subsided and all was calm. "Where is **YOUR** faith?" He asked.

His words touched my soul and, almost immediately, I would begin to feel God's presence. In awe, I would experience the calming of the Holy Spirit which reminded me of the time when Jesus calmed the sea. When the storm came up and the boat began to be tossed about, the disciples frantically called out to Jesus, "Master, master, we are sinking!"

He had been there for the disciples in their weak faith, and now He was here for **ME.** This was the peace I had been seeking when I said, "That's okay God."

"He *IS* here," I said, feeling *His* strength -- His very breath -- pouring into me. This supernatural feeling changed my negative attitude to one of joy and acceptance. "Don, you're right. God is in this very room!" It was a victorious moment for both of us.

The doctors continued to use their medical skills in an effort to help Don, but the cancer was relentlessly moving in for the final attack. His physical condition continued to deteriorate. Everything was being stripped from him except the marvelous faith that held him, like an invisible wire, to God's throne.

9

WHY?

Why did Don have to die? . . . The nurse's voice brought me out of my thoughts and back to the present reality of Don's death. "Is there something I can do for you?" she asked kindly.

"No -- there's nothing." *What could anyone do now? It was over -- the long fight was over. My husband had taken the train to heaven, leaving me behind!*

Once again, I sought some explanation. "Oh, God, why? Please make me understand why!"

Today, two years later, there are still unanswered questions in my heart and the hearts of others. We wonder why it is that some experience their divine healing here on earth, while others receive the ultimate healing by going to be with their Savior. Many people, in an effort to show kindness, would offer various comments such as: *It is God's will that*

Don be with Him. Perhaps God was sparing him from some future danger or temptation. Everyone has to die -- it was his time.

None of these well-intentioned thoughts help much when you have just lost your spouse. The "why" remains, but I do know that God permits things to happen -- God, who created all things -- is in control of all things and nothing happens by chance. In Romans 8:28 we read, "And we know that all things work together *for good* to them that love God, to them who are called according to His *purpose.*" As a Christian, I believe, according to this Scripture, that one day we will be able to look back and understand why God permitted certain things to happen. We will see the "for good" and the "purpose."

I believe Don and I prayed in earnest faith. We felt we could have transformed the entire Rocky Mountain range from west to east, but the cancer didn't move. Don't healing was not impossible for God -- He did not fail, nor did we. God drew my husband to Him, according to His plan and purpose.

I also believe there are times when God gives individuals a supernatural gift of faith which overcomes all barriers to healing. God may choose to give this gift to a person for a specific time and/or purpose. When this happens, the person steps out of their human limitations and into the dimension of Almighty God.

No, I don't have the answer to the "**why**" but I think about I Peter 1:4-7 which reads:

> And God has reserved for His children the priceless gift of eternal life; it is kept in heaven for you, pure and undefiled, beyond the reach of change and decay. And God, in His mighty power, will make sure that you get there safely to receive it, because you are trusting in Him. It will be yours in that

coming day for all to see. So be truly glad! There is wonderful joy ahead, even though the going is rough for a while down here.

These trials are only to test your faith, to see whether or not it is strong and pure. It is being tested as fire tests gold and purifies it -- and your faith is far more precious to God than mere gold; so if your faith remains strong after being tried in the test tube of fiery trials, it will bring you much praise and glory and honor on the day of His return.

The writer, Peter, is saying that we should trust even though we may not receive the answers until Christ appears. I may not totally understand why my husband wasn't healed until I stand face to face with God but, in the meantime, I am learning to rely on Him for the "peace that passes all understanding." We are all just passing through this life, but the things of God are eternal.

I thought about how the children would be affected by the loss of their father. The children, each in their own way, would have to deal with the situation. The doctors said we would need to draw strength from one another. Somehow I knew that God would sustain us in our grief.

I remember how our daughter Judy had been there at the hospital helping Don every way she could. She would bring his favorite food, trying to induce an appetite that had vanished. Don would try his best to eat -- just to please her. Judy would also feed him spiritually -- reading Scriptures that ministered to both of them.

Because they were so close, Don was open with her in talking about his death. "What do you feel about me dying?" he had asked.

Remembering Judy's response, brought me comfort -- even now. She said, "Dad, you won't walk here on earth; but you will be made whole in God's kingdom."

Don smiled, realizing she accpted the fact that he was dying.

Andy was devastated when he first learned of his father's cancer. He still needed his father's love, companionship, and advice. But as Don grew weaker in body, Andy became stronger in his faith. God had been slowly paving the way for this time of testing. Don's death, I was sure, would make Andy's relationship with God even stronger.

My role in our son's life had changed dramatically, Always in the past, he had relied on me; but, during those last few months, I had reached out to him. We were relating as one adult to another.

Pete, our son-in-law, was a blessing to us through the many months of illness. Every morning, prior to going to work, he would come over to pray and reassure us.

"He's going to be okay," he would tell me. "Don't cry."

Like me, he asked questions. He wanted to know why "this" was happening -- why "that" wasn't happening.

Andy's wife, Suzanne, was always a blessing and joy to me. I thought of her as a daughter and grew to appreciate her as a light in our family. She had clung to the fact that Don was going to "make it."

One morning she called me. "Mom, I had a dream that Don was healed. I just know it's going to happen."

I told her that was great. I wanted to believe it but, at that particular time, was struggling with doubts.

The kids called Don "Pap Pap." When he would have a rough night, Suzanne and I would share our tears -- she for Pap Pap, I for my husband. This drew us closer together.

When I needed a change of clothes, Judy would go to our house and select an outfit to bring to me at the hospital where I had set up camp. Spotting her armload of "presents," Don would remark, "It sure looks like Christmas." I could always count on my daughter to be there with her gift of love.

Tina and her father had a remarkable relationship. She really had a talent for bringing the humor out of him. She was his "fashion" critic. Don would always change a tie or jacket whenever she told him it didn't look right.

"Get with it, Dad," she would say. "This generation is passing you by!"

I knew Tina would have a great deal of difficulty in dealing with her father's death. She would miss him terribly -- but as a believer in the Word -- she would make it.

Yes, Don was gone; but I thank God for my family. Now I had to tell them about their father's death. "Help them, God; help all of us."

10

PREPARATIONS

Jesus tells us in John 14:2,3 that "There are many homes up there where my Father lives, and I am going to prepare them for your coming. When everything is ready, then I will come and get you, so that you can always be with me where I am. If this weren't so, I would tell you plainly." Yes, He has prepared Heaven for our arrival. Since the beginning of time, God has been making preparations for us to share in His kingdom.

From the moment of birth, our mind expands with knowledge and our spirit grows stronger -- but our physical body begins to die. God intended that man spend eternity with Him in His kingdom; this is our inheritance as His children.

We become part of God's kingdom the moment we accept Jesus as our Savior. Learning to walk daily with the Lord and trusting Him in all situations is part of our growth process. We should try to pattern our lives after Jesus and -- in a way -- also our death. Our physical body dies but we have the power of His resurrection which gives us new life. Philippians 1:21 says, "For to me, living means opportunities for Christ, and dying -- well, that's better yet."

Through Christ, God prepared the way for us to enter into Heaven. However, we, as individuals, also need to prepare for our exit from this earth by accepting His sacrifice for our salvation. Then there are earthly, practical matters to take care of while we are still alive. Have you made a will? Have you made your intentions clear about life support systems and heroic measures to keep you alive? How do you feel about the donation of your organs to help others? Would you want to have an autopsy? Are your important legal documents in a safety deposit box or other place accessible to family members? Have you told them where they are located?

From personal experience, I learned that if possible, a husband and wife should discuss and pre-plan their funeral and burial arrangements. When Don was near death, my sister-in-law, with much tact, asked me if she could help by making arrangements for Don's burial. I thanked her for her concern and, although I didn't want to believe my husband was dying, I gave her the finances to take care of the arrangements. If Don had made his wishes known to me, it would have been easier to deal with the emotional aspects of planning his funeral. I have found that there are many "forethought" or "pre-paid" funeral plans available from which a person can choose. Participants make all selections and arrangements in advance of their death, saving their loved ones the pain of possibly making an incorrect, and sometimes costly, decision in their grief . . .

At the funeral home as I looked down at Don for the first time, he appeared just as he had before the illness. There was no pain etched on his face, no visible effects of the cancer on his body -- the funeral director had done an excellent job of preparing him. My heart ached seeing him there, but peace came to me when I realized that he was absent from the body and present with the Lord. This body looked like Don but it was just an empty shell that had housed his indomitable spirit -- he wasn't here -- he was at complete peace with Jesus. The certainty of knowing exactly where Don was, sustained me through all the tears and heartache.

Many friends and relatives came to see Don at the funeral home. Their caring presence brought a great deal of comfort to me. The room was always crowded, but I felt all alone in a world that my husband had just left. I could feel God's love through the people, but my heart still felt a void that I knew would never be filled here on earth. I shall only be fulfilled completely when, in eternity, I will once again see Don, standing with Jesus.

11

TUNNEL OF GRIEVING

Now that Don was gone, the next period of my life would be a fight for emotional survival as I searched for undertanding, a way to deal with my grief, and a reason to go on living. Although I'd say, "That's okay, God," living with the reality and finality of Don's death was painful beyond words.

The first stage of my grieving had begun when the nurse told me that I had to let Don go. That had been difficult but the experiences and stages yet to come would test my sanity. I would go up and down an emotional ladder of despair, loneliness, self-pity and frustration. During this time I longed for comfort; yet, I kept the true Comforter at a distance, inwardly protesting what He had allowed to happen.

As the days passed, I asked over and over again why I had given up -- why I hadn't begged Don to hold on -- to keep fighting. I thought about Don's medical treatment -- maybe we should have taken him to other specialists, to other well-known treatment centers. Perhaps there was a prayer I didn't pray. Was there a special diet that could have helped? I now realize that asking -- "What could have been done differently?" -- is a normal part of the grieving process. Often the surviving family members feel guilty because they are still alive, so they punish themselves with self-blame.

God didn't tell me what He was going to do with me now that Don was gone and I was left behind. It seemed as though He didn't care that my heart was breaking. I was lonely and scared and, somehow, I felt as if it were all God's fault. He had promised never to leave me, but I no longer trusted His promises. Would this horrible, empty feeling ever go away?

It is devastating to face the realization that a marriage partner is gone from your life. I would awaken during the night, expecting to find Don beside me but, instead, there was just empty space. How desperately I wanted to hear his voice, to touch his hand, to share his thoughts. Oh, the terrible wave of tears and loneliness that would engulf me...

It would have been easy to give up -- to retreat from life and simply wait out the number of days I had left. Some people do this, while others spend their remaining time engaged in a flurry of meaningless activity. Both of these routes are attempts to escape from the reality of a broken heart. I knew I had to find my purpose for being left behind -- for being left in the harvest field.

When I left the hospital and went home without Don, I realized the house would never again be the same for me. Within its walls were very painful reminders of something that was gone forever. There were Don's clothes, his fishing gear, his toolboxes -- all bits and pieces of his life. *Maybe I should sell the house,* I thought. *It might be easier to forget -- but I don't want to forget. Oh, God, it's so confusing. So overwhelming!*

I remembered what Don said about keeping the house and I decided to do as he had suggested -- at least for then. It wasn't easy! Separated from Don, I felt like an intruder in the dwelling that had been our haven for so many years. No house ever seemed so large, nor so empty. Of course, it helped to have Tina, our youngest daughter, with me. I don't think I would have been able to stay there without her.

After the funeral, family and friends frequently came to the house to visit. But after awhile these visits slowed down; people had their own lives to live. The loneliness was hard to take -- so very hard. I used television, traveling and reading to fill the void, but found them to be only momentary distractions. They could not fulfill the basic human requirements of being loved, feeling needed, and belonging.

God could have filled my emptiness but I refused to ask anything of Him. When I tried to pray, I ended up lashing out at Him with accusations about His fairness. Where was His explanation.

For nearly six months, I stayed away from church because I did not want to hear about faith, healing, and God's promises to His children. The Scriptures that had helped Don and me during his illness, now caused me to cry in grief. It was so difficult to function normally; despair was eating away at my very soul.

I discovered that walking helped ease my tension. Some type of exercise is good therapy for dealing with grief. A friend of mine, Jeanne Anderson, usually walked with me, and would encourage me with her uplifting words. "You are doing okay," she insisted. "You're going to make it."

As we walked, I would carry on a one-sided, silent conversation with God. It wasn't communication, though, because I wasn't expecting to receive any answers -- and, of course, I didn't. My spirit was rebelling -- and yet it hungered for that very thing that the enemy was trying to steal. My walking continued; sometimes I would walk as many as eight miles a day. At this point, my exercise had become an obsessive outlet, rather than a healthy one.

Jeanne spoke frankly to me one day. "Don't you think it's time to leave this pit of despair and enter into the tunnel of recovery? One may get temporarily stuck in the tunnel, and that's okay, as long as they continue toward the light of Jesus Christ."

Her words witnessed to me. I thought about the many others who were concerned. Judy Nelson, my encourager, would often meet with me for breakfast and to share Scripture with me. Other friends were standing in faith as prayer warriors. The words of Frank and Nina (friends who often came to my home to share Christ's teachings) began to take hold in my spirit. This dedicated couple was blessed with a special understanding of Scripture and conveyed it with such faith and joy that it was impossible not to respond. Then there were the visits and calls from various pastors who had taken an interest in Don's condition. Now they expressed their concern for me. I knew that my children, amidst their own pain, were also praying for me non-stop.

How I love and appreciate all these wonderful people! Their prayers made the difference, and my heart began to slowly mend. I began to ask God for forgiveness for my negative attitude toward Him. I wanted to feel His comforting Presence -- I wanted to trust Him again. In order to find the peace and healing I was aching for, I realized that I needed to ask God to forgive me for being angry with Him.

When I finally began to feel more comfortable living in the house without Don, I knew that it was progress. Perhaps it was happening because I was starting to feel the reality of God coming back into my life. I realized I could never be alone -- not with Jesus as my companion. I like my home and it's a nice place to be. After all, my husband provided this place for me to live. Until I join him in our heavenly mansion, it will do just fine.

When Don was in the hospital, I lost weight. It wasn't easy for me to concentrate on food when my husband had no appetite and could eat very little. Then, after his death, it didn't seem to matter whether I ate or not. Who cared?

Throughout the years, Don had always come home for lunch -- something I looked forward to. Now, I'd listen for the door to pop open, half-expecting to hear him say, "What's for lunch? I'm starved." But, of course, this wasn't going to happen -- not ever again.

Friends would say, "Mary, you have to eat, you're going to be sick."

I appreciated their concern, but felt that my health didn't matter.

At first it was depression that had taken away my appetite but, later, it was my own rebellion. I never had any control over whether Don lived or died, but I could have some control over my own fate. When I thought about my appearance, I felt the same kind of frustration . . . Who cared? There was nobody to dress up for. Nobody cared whether or not I got my hair done. Why bother doing it for myself -- whoever that was?

This led to the next stage of grieving which I call my "identity crisis." I had always been introduced as Dr. Virostek's wife but now I was a *widow*. I hated the sound of that word and couldn't accept what it meant. I didn't belong anywhere; I was no longer special to someone. Independence was a foreign feeling to me.

In time, God began to reveal that I could be independent by being dependent on Him. My true identity began to unravel as I once again began to think of myself as a child of God. The pain lessened but the loneliness was still difficult to deal with.

Dr. Craig W. Ellison, a Christian psychologist and author of LONELINESS, THE SEARCH FOR INTIMACY, states that Christians are the least lonely of all people. He says, "All humans need intimacy, and ultimate intimacy depends upon finding, knowing, and sharing God. We need each other but others can never be enough. As we establish and deepen our relationship with God, we'll experience a sense of communication and acceptance that people and events can't destroy."

Until I became a widow, I never realized that the world seems to be made for couples. I felt like a puzzle piece that didn't fit in anywhere -- like a fifth wheel. Although there is still a friendship with those couples with whom my husband and I were friends, it just isn't the same. There is a missing face. Sometimes I find myself wanting to tell couples to take time to appreciate one another. Tomorrows are uncertain! I want to tell them to talk -- to touch -- to love -- unconditionally.

Christmas and other holidays are the worst! I keep remembering how things used to be for Don and me -- the way we celebrated an occasion -- our special traditions. There seems little reason to "deck the halls" now, but, because of the rest of my family, I have to try. The first time I actually found myself enjoying a festive moment without Don, I was shocked; then I relaxed, knowing that this is what Don would have wanted. With God's help, I am confident that it will get easier. Isaiah 26:3 tells me that, "He will keep in perfect peace all those who trust in Him, whose thoughts turn often to the Lord! Trust in the Lord God always, for in the Lord Jehovah is your everlasting strength."

It is this trust which helps me attain my independence and freedom to be myself in Christ. Don had been the spiritual leader of our household; now I found myself in this unfamiliar role. An example of this is when I attended a single's group and prayed for other individuals who were hurting physically and spiritually.

Don had been the head of our family. I had relied on him to make the major decisions while I enjoyed my position as wife and helpmate. But at this point, like it or not, I am compelled to say, "Now, the buck stops here! Mary, you have to take charge." When the kids want parental advice -- it will have to come from me. The household bills, previously paid by Don, are now my responsibiltiy. It has become my sole decision concerning all purchases made -- from breakfast cereal to a new car. Every day I become more aware of the responsibilities that go with being a widow, but with this awareness comes increasing confidence. I find myself saying, **"That's okay God"** -- as I am given new problems to overcome in my goal for independence.

12

A VICTORIOUS LANDING

Practical, day by day experiences of normal life -- that's what it's all about, really, isn't it? Living. Loving. Having children. Being with family and friends. Going on picnics. Going to church. Reading the Bible. Holding hands. Going on a moonlight drive or a walk through the park. Caring. Sharing. Laughter. Tears. Life. Death.

Don faced life's experiences triumphantly, as a man of faith and love. I, too, have experienced all of these things except one and that shall come in due time. But in the meantime, I have, through the living presence of Christ in my life, learned to cope with grief. I have learned to think about tomorrow and anticipate its happenings with joy.

After Don died, there was a period of time when I avoided places that we used to frequent. For a while

I didn't want to go into public places. Well-meaning people would come up and say, "Oh, you poor thing. It's such a shame... He was so young -- such a good person ... I miss him."

Then I would say, "So do I," and talk about my yesterdays. But now I say, "So do I. But let me tell you what's new in my life -- how excited I am about the victory I have experienced through God's love."

Other times, friends would tell me that they had been thinking about contacting me in regard to various social programs designed to help people cope with the loss of a spouse. When this happened I would want to turn away because I didn't want to be labeled a *widow*. It was too final! Don was gone! People didn't have their friend and favorite dentist, and I didn't have my husband.

Now I say, "Thank you for caring. Let's get together and you can tell me about it."

Weekends without Don were especially difficult for me. My children would invite me to their homes for dinner. Friends would also try to include me in their weekend plans. At first I didn't want to go anywhere, and would refuse their invitations. Now I say, "Thank you," and, if I'm free, I go expecting to enjoy myself with people who care. It's called "coping with grief." The pain is less devastating. The Lord is working it out *in* me -- and *for* me -- in spite of myself.

To exercise my body and clear my thoughts, I continue to walk every day. I see so much of God in nature. For awhile my walks were mostly for therapy; now they are mostly for fun.

God is the reason for my recovery. He has been there all along -- even when I was angrily withdrawing from Him. Now, He is beginning to use me to reach out to other people who are hurting from the separation or loss of a loved one. Don was right when he said God would give me a special ministry;

He has opened more and more doors for me.

Two years ago I attended a Christian Writers' workshop with a friend. When she asked me to go, I was hesitant. "You write poetry," I said, "but I've never written anything."

"But you've said you would like to write a book about Don -- a book which could help others. Maybe you'll make some good contacts."

Although I agreed to go, I wasn't convinced it was a good idea. Nothing really interested me -- nothing offered a challenge to my mind. It was still easier to live on memories and, maybe once in a while, talk vaguely about something I'd like to do.

Going to that workshop changed my life. God used it to give me a sense of direction -- a spark of interest in something pertaining to the future. That evening, our Lord began building a foundation from which would grow a ministry of helping the grieving and broken-hearted.

Everything the publisher said interested me, and I found myself searching in my purse for a pencil and paper so that I could take notes. The Holy Spirit was drawing me toward these people -- toward this company. Writing my book was suddenly more than a possibility; it was a reality.

A few days later, God paved the way for me to personally meet the publisher who had conducted the workshop. When I told her about my desire to write a book concerning my relationship with my husband, she encouraged me to go ahead with the project. Although she could not promise publication, she said that their editorial staff would review it upon completion. I thanked God for what He had brought about, since I learned at the workshop that less than one percent of all manuscripts which come into a publisher's office ever get printed. Realizing that I was limited in my talents as a writer, I contracted to have a professional writer assist me.

When the manuscript was completed, the editorial board accepted it for publication. As I began working with the staff of Rainbow's End, it seemed clear that Satan was placing obstacles in our way to stop the book from being printed. For example, there were unexpected demands on our time, health problems, and personal family matters which interfered with progress. However, our Lord, the Author of all life, would not be silenced; and we praise Him for bringing us together for His purposes and glory. When we thought we were ready to publish the book, we really weren't -- it had to be God's timing. There were additional chapters of my life which had not yet been lived.

So much is happening! When I was asked to speak at a banquet in New Kensington, I couldn't believe anyone would really want to hear anything I had to say. But they listened -- and they apparently liked what they heard. Since then, I have been asked to speak at churches, workshops, seminars, and single's groups. I have even appeared on television. God is good!

When I speak, the Lord usually has me talk about life with Don -- the cancer battle that was fought and lost -- my grieving and struggle for independence -- the ultimate victory that was found in Jesus. Many people tell me my words have helped them in their own grief. They know, because I've experienced it, that I can relate to their feelings. When they see that I am, once again, responding to the challenges of life, they are encouraged.

Yes, I've truly worked through -- **landed** -- in my grief. I realized this the day I moved Don's favorite chair back into the family room. When Don died, someone had shoved it into a corner of the living room, believing it would upset me to see it in its familiar spot, obviously empty.

Eventually the day came when I noticed the chair ... *Why wasn't it where it belonged? Why was no one sitting in it?* These questions brought about the realization that I needed to release other "things" to God (as well as my grief) so that healing could continue. Don's chair was comfortable to sit in and it matched the decor in the family room, so I triumphantly moved it back where it belonged. After all, Don didn't need it now! He had a wonderfully comfortable chair in Heaven at the banquet table with the King of Kings. I smiled, visualizing the empty chair reserved beside him. It is mine!

How different my life is as a widow. *Yes, I'm using that horrible word.* Don, in his chair, looking down from heaven, must be saying, "Is that really my Mary? The hospital volunteer -- the writer and newsletter editor -- the public speaker -- the T.V. personality. **She's so independent!** Yes this is the woman I loved and will love throughout all eternity -- the woman I am so proud of. Yes, he'd say, that's definitely my Mary. **And that's okay, God.**"

About Donald Virostek . . .

Don Virostek was born February 19, 1931 in East Vandergrift, Pennsylvania. He and Mary, his wife, lived in Vandergrift until his death on February 8, 1988. Don was a loving husband as well as the supportive, caring father of one son and two daughters. As a devout Christian, Don's life reflected what Jesus is all about. He was a "giving" person, always concerned about the needs of others.

Growing up in a country town, Don enjoyed hunting, fishing and sports. In 1949 he graduated from Vandergrift High School -- after proving his ability on the basketball court. His college friends from the University of Pittsburgh remember him as quiet, unassuming, and intellectual.

Although Don's dental practice was successful, he was even more successful as a "person." He was appreciated and respected by his family, friends, and collegues.

Don belonged to three organizations in his life -- Sigma Delta Sigma, the American Dental Association, and St. Gertrude's Church. He won many awards, both as a scholar and athlete; when he got involved in something he always gave it his *total* effort.

In 1953 the use of oxygen in sports was introduced at the University of Pittsburgh. Several top, national magazines found this to be newsworthy, reporting that the idea was not to "supercharge" the athletes, but to help them recover more quickly from fatigue. Oxygen was administered during rest periods. It was supplied through a mask attached to a compact, portable unit called the Vitalator, consisting of a refillable 40 cubic foot oxygen cylinder mounted in a light frame with handle. Don's picture, showing him wearing the mask and sniffing oxygen, was featured in *life* magazine.

At the 21st Annual Inductions Ceremonies, Dr. Donald Virostek was inducted into the Allegheny-Kiski Valley Sports Hall of Fame. Don set three rebounding records at Pitt (1952-53); single game (26), average per game (20.2) and season (424 in 24 games). The latter was broken by Jerome Lane, with 444 in 33 games, but the others still stand. Honors bestowed on Don include: Pitt Athletic Committee Awardee, AP All-State Team, and Pittsburgh Press Collegiate Player of the Year Award. His name was inscribed on Pitt's Varsity Walk, signifying "high scholar-athlete" status. Mary Virostek accepted the award on behalf of her husband.

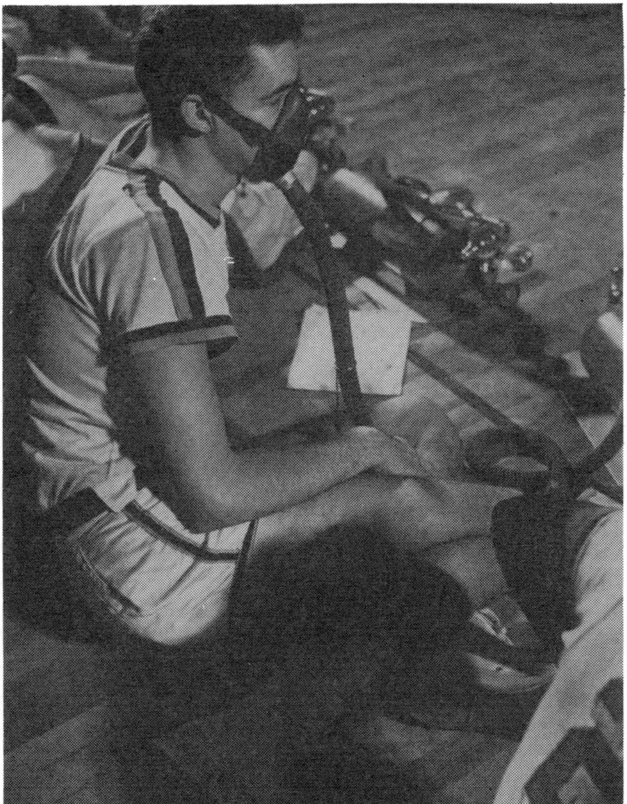

REFLECTIONS

"It was through Don's participation in the prayer meetings at St. Gertrude's Church that I came to know him as a man of faith with deep personal feelings for God. Don was not a Scripture scholar, nor was he a theologian, but his comments on the Scripture readings were enlightening and inspirational, relating to everyday life. He was a man who loved God, loved the Word of God, and loved his fellow brothers and sisters.

"When Don became seriously ill, I began to take Holy Communion to him. Although I could see the effects of his disease and knew he was in pain, never once did I hear him complain.

"On February 8, 1988, Don died. Knowing the depth of his faith, I am sure that Don met his God with the same deep, religious conviction that sustained him in life. Three days later, I celebrated the Mass of Christian Burial for him. In faith, I am convinced that Don Virostek is walking hand in hand with the Lord, his Savior -- the Jesus he loved so much during the time he lived among us."

> Reverend Marion R. Gallo, OSB
> Saint Gertrude Church
> Vandergrift, Pa.

"Working with Dr. Virostek for twelve years made a deep impression on my life. He was a soft-spoken gentle man with a wonderful sense of humor. His deep devotion to his family and religion could be clearly seen."

> Marge Ferraro
> Pittsburgh, Pa.

"It was a wonderful three years that I worked for Don Virostek. His sharing the Good News and witnessing about Jesus to patients and staff probably reached more people in his short life than I'll reach in my lifetime."

> Mary Curry
> Apollo, Pa.

"I remember Don's child-like faith and found this personally refreshing and proof that the *wind* of the Holy Spirit *blows where it wills*. I saw Don gain the victory, first in his spiritual life, and later in his illness."

> Pastor Rodney Murray
> 1st Presbyterian Church
> Vandergrift, Pa.

"There are many things I remember about Don but one thing in particular stands out -- his special baseball hat with the words *"Jesus said he would"* printed on the front. He was a man of tremendous faith, leaving behind a lot of people who will always remember him."

> William "Bill" Naccarato
> Vandergrift, Pa.

"Prior to Don's illness he had a strong personal relationship with Jesus; however, it was during his battle with cancer when we saw a strength and boldness that wasn't there before -- a strength in the knowledge that Jesus was always there and a boldness to be a witness of God's love and mercy to others."

> Don and Marilyn Scalzott
> Greensburg, Pa.

"If I have learned only one lesson in my seventeen year friendship with Don Virostek -- it is to take the time now to enjoy life. The experience has been rewarding to know such a marvelous person."

> Harold J. Samay, D.D.S.
> New Kensington, Pa.

"Don Virostek became a close friend during college. He had a sense of humor and a lot of courage. As a person trained in medicine, he knew that there are many ways to die. He accepted the inevitable outcome of his illness and died with dignity and grace. In his unselfish way he showed concern and compassion to his family and friends, trying to hide his pain and severity of the illness. You can't help but love someone like that -- someone who cares more about others than himself."

> Michael Zernich, M.D.
> Aliquippa, Pa.

"I feel blessed that my family and I got to know Don as a man who loved God with tremendous faith and wisdom. It is hard to find words that do justice in describing how he lived and shared that faith with others. I am thankful my children got to know Don and love him. I pray the memory of his strong faith and values will stay in their minds forever."

> Betsy Boland
> Vandergrift, Pa.

"Don had a sweetness about him that could be compared to the results of a chocolate bar dropped on a sidewalk on a warm summer's day. He could simply melt into any given situation and, at the same time, draw people like ants. He indeed was a man of warmth and character, and he was human."

> Pastor Tom Walters
> Word of Life Ministries
> Jeanette, Pa.

"Don was a true Christian, in that he could not only forgive, but could also forget. He showed love and hospitality toward all. He was concerned about others even when he was ill. I am sure many came to Jesus through Don's illness."

> Jean Poti
> Manassas, Va.

"We always felt uplifted by Don's ready smile when we visited him in the hospital. Don loved Jesus in a special way -- a way we should all desire."

> Dave and Judy Nelson
> Leechburg, Pa.

"Don will always be a part of our lives, just as he was part of our most joyous memories...He was the most special and humble man we have ever known. We were privileged to have him as a personal friend and believe everyone who had this same opportunity was also richly blessed. His gentle, loving spirit was a ray of sunshine in this trying world."

Bruce and Vivian Bish
Greensburg, Pa.

"We saw Don as a gentle giant, a man of great accomplishment, but with a humble spirit and a cloak of humility. When Don realized his salvation through Jesus, he was blessed with a hunger and thirst for spiritual things. We will always remember him as a man who tried to live in a way that would please God."

Don and Jeannie Anderson
Apollo, Pa.

"What we remember most about Don was his excitement and the joy that you saw on his face as he spoke of Jesus coming again. In sickness and in health, you saw Jesus in Don Virostek."

Fran and Dee Raymond
Houston, Texas

DONALD VIROSTEK'S FAVORITE BIBLE VERSES

(Quoted from the Living Bible)

Note: These life-giving Scriptures strengthened Don as he battled cancer. He realized that, in Christ, death was defeated and the ultimate victory was his, regardless of what happened to his earthly body.

I Corinthians 15:51-57 -- But I am telling you this strange and wonderful secret: we shall not all die, but we shall all be given new bodies! It will all happen in a moment, in the twinkling of an eye, when the last trumpet is blown. For there will be a trumpet blast from the sky and all the Christians who have died will suddenly become alive, with new bodies that will never, never die; and then we who are still alive shall suddenly have new bodies, too. For our earthly bodies, the ones we have now that can die, must be transformed into heavenly bodies that cannot perish but will live forever.

When this happens, then at last this Scripture will come true -- Death is swallowed up in victory. O death, where then your victory? Where then your sting? For sin -- the sting that causes death -- will all be gone; and the law, which reveals our sins, will no longer be our judge. How we thank God for all of this! It is He who makes us victorious through Jesus Christ our Lord!

2 Corinthians 2:15,16 -- As far as God is concerned there is a sweet, wholesome fragrance in our lives. It is the fragrance of Christ within us, an aroma to both the saved and the unsaved all around us. To those who are not being saved, we seem a fearful smell of death and doom, while to those who know Christ we are a life giving perfume.

Galatians 2:20 -- I have been crucified with Christ; and I myself no longer live, but Christ lives in me. And the real life I now have within this body is a result of my trusting in the Son of God, who loved me and gave Himself for me.

Hebrews 13:5,6 -- For God has said, I will never, never fail you nor forsake you. That is why we can say without any doubt or fear, The Lord is my Helper and I am not afraid of anything that mere man can do to me.

Isaiah 26:3,4 -- He will keep in perfect peace all those who trust in Him, whose thoughts turn often to the Lord. Trust in the Lord God always, for in the Lord Jehovah is your everlasting strength.

Isaiah 30:20 -- Though He give you the bread of adversity and water of affliction, yet He will be with you to teach you -- with your own eyes you will see your Teacher.

Isaiah 40:29 -- He gives power to the tired and worn out, and strength to the weak.

Isaiah 41:10 -- Fear not, for I am with you. Do not be dismayed. I am your God. I will strengthen you; I will help you; I will uphold you with my victorious right hand.

Isaiah 41:13 -- I am holding you by your right hand -- I, the Lord your God -- and I say to you, Don't be afraid; I am here to help you.

Isaiah 53:7 -- He was oppressed and He was afflicted, yet He never said a word. He was brought as a lamb to the slaughter; and as a sheep before her shearers is dumb, so He stood silent before the ones condemning Him.

John 3:16 -- For God loved the world so much that He gave His only Son so that anyone who believes in Him shall not perish but have eternal life.

I John 4:12 -- For though we have never yet seen God, when we love each other God lives in us and His love within us grows ever stronger.

I John 4:18 -- We need have no fear of someone who loves us perfectly; His perfect love for us eliminates all dread of what He might do to us.

Job 23:10 -- But He knows every detail of what is happening to me; and when He has examined me, He will pronounce me completely innocent -- as pure as solid gold!

Luke 9:24,25 -- Whoever loses his life for my sake will save it, but whoever insists on keeping his life will lose it; and what profit is there in gaining the whole world when it means forfeiting one's self?

Luke 12:31 -- He will always give you all you need from day to day if you will make the Kingdom of God your primary concern.

Matthew 11:28 -- Come to me and I will give you rest -- all of you work so hard beneath a heavy yoke.

Matthew 17:20 -- For if you had faith even as small as a tiny mustard seed you could say to this mountain "Move" and it would go far away. Nothing would be impossible.

Nahum 1:7 -- The Lord is good. When trouble comes, He is the place to go! And He knows everyone who trusts in Him.

I Peter 3:18 -- Christ also suffered. He died once for the sins of us guilty sinners, although He Himself was innocent of any sin at any time, that He might bring us safely home to God.

Philippians 4:13 -- For I can do everything God asks me to with the help of Christ who gives me the strength and power.

Philippians 4:19 -- And it is He who will supply all your needs from His riches in glory, because of what Christ has done for us.

Proverbs 2:8 -- He grants good sense to the godly -- His saints. He is their shield, protecting them and guarding their pathway.

Psalm 9:9 -- All who are oppressed may come to Him. He is a refuge for them in their times of trouble.

Psalm 16:11 -- You have let me experience the joys of life and the exquisite pleasures of your own eternal presence.

Psalm 23:4 -- Even when walking through the dark valley of death I will not be afraid, for You are close beside me, guarding, guiding all the way.

Psalm 31:7 -- I am radiant with joy because of Your mercy, for You have listened to my troubles and have seen the crisis in my soul.

Psalm 37:23 -- The steps of good men are directed by the Lord. He delights in each step they take. If they fall it isn't fatal, for the Lord holds them with His hand.

Psalm 40:1,2 -- I waited patiently for God to help me; then He listened and heard my cry. He lifted me out of the pit of despair, out from the bog and the mire, and set my feet on a hard, firm path and steadied me as I walked along.

Revelation 21:4 -- He will wipe away all tears from their eyes, and there shall be no more death, nor sorrow, nor crying, nor pain. All of that has gone forever.

Romans 5:3 -- We can rejoice, too, when we run into problems and trials for we know that they are good for us -- they help us learn to be patient.

I Thessalonians 4:13,14 -- An now, dear brothers, I want you to know what happens to a Christian when he dies so that when it happens, you will not be full of sorrow, as those are who have no hope. For since we believe that Jesus died and then came back to life again, we can also believe that when Jesus returns, God will bring back with Him all the Christians who have died.

II Timothy 2:3 -- Take your share of suffering as a good soldier of Jesus Christ, just as I do, and as Christ's soldier do not let yourself become tied up in worldly affairs, for then you cannot satisfy the one who has enlisted you in His army.

EPILOGUE

God is so good! Recently, He gave us a very special gift. On January 21, 1990, Donald Jacob Virostek, our first grandson, was born to Andy's wife Suzanne. How I wish Don could have been here to share this special moment with us and to watch his namesake grow into manhood. But, we, his family, have victory in knowing that Don is in Heaven with the Giver of Life, rejoicing with us.

A special "thank you" to everyone who provided loving support and care to Don and our entire family, during his illness and beyond . . .

Our apologies to anyone whose name we may have inadvertently omitted from this list.

Dan and Patty Alberts
Mark Alberts
Rose Albini
Dorothy Altman
Dr. Ted and Rosemarie Altman
and Family
Bill and Marlene Ament
Don and Jeanne Anderson
and Family
Bud and Fran Armitage
Dorothy Arteritano
Fred and Evelyn Baker and Family
Joe and Rhonda Beasley
Eugenie Bell
Betty Benes
Robert and Nancy Berberich
Bob and Vera Beuten
Dennis and Debbie Biagioni
and girls
Tony Bione and Family
Bruce and Vivian Bish
Pete and Helen Blaizes
Joseph and Betsy Boland and Family
Madeline Breznican
Dutch and Georgia Burch and Family
Pastor Billy Burke
Robert and Sally Burns
Frank and Nina Cain
Eugene Calderazzo
Gloria Calderazzo
George and Barb Capretto
Teresa Carrara
Blanche Carricato
Dennis and Jennifer Caveglia
Pastor Bob Caviness
Argie, Evelyn and Irene Ceraso
Frances and Edith Ceraso

Dr. Frank and Rita Ceraso and Family
John and Polly Ceraso
Sue Ceraso
Sylvia Ceraso
Tom and Janet Cersaso
Joseph and Gen Chechak
Bob and Peg Chelko
Mary Cheris
Paul and Alice Chieffalo
Dean and Evelyn Cline and Family
Bill and Mary Colaianni
Ruth Colaianni
Ben and Rose Colantonio and Family
Jeff and Joyce Cortileso and Family
Dr. Bob and Mary Coy
Dom and Ann Cristello
Michael Cucchiara and Family
Dr. Jack and Cindy Cullen and Family
Grace Curtis and Family
Furman and Mary Curry and Family
Ben and Gloria DeBiasio
John and Lucy DeBiasio
Rose DeBiasio and Family
Santo and Betty Debiasio
Ann DeCola and Family
Gino and Rita DeFrancisis
Verna Mae Delia
Bob and Peiere Delledonne
Dennis and Patty Delledonne
Sil and Margaret DeLuca and Family
Sister Benita DeMattis
Al and Rose DeMichele
Angie Demolin
Loretta Dentzel
Tony and Arlene DePansis
and Family

Guido and Carmella DePaul
  and Family
Nick and Betty DePetris
Anna DeSalvo
Christy and Ninnie DeSalvo
  and Family
Ray and Edith Detman
Alfred and Theresa Dettore
John Dettore
Lillian Doonis and Family
Ed and Joan Dovyack
Jerry and Laureen Dropka
  and Family
Sister Eleanor
Joe and Lilly Errante and Family
Jerry and Darla Everhardt
Angie Faiola and Family
Marino and Theresa Fasano
  and Family
Jerry and Debbie Ferencak
  and Family
Jim and Lee Ferraccio
John and Ann Ferraccio
Bob and Norma Ferrara
Aurelio and Tessie Ferraro
  and Family
Louis and and Ann Ferraro
Louis and Naomi Ferraro
Marge Ferraro
Joe and Theresa Fontana
Bud and Marge Forinash
Greg Forman
Arthur and Violet Gallo
Frank and Loretta Gallo
Father Marion Gallo
Victoria Gallo
Dave and Lori Geogvich and Family
Mark and Helen Grana
Tony and Nancy Graziano
Gertrude "Sweetsie" Gustafson
Betty Heckman
Bob and Judy Heim and Family
Gene and Helen Highfield
Carol Holben
Paul and Patty Hollinger
Paul and Anne Horvat
Omer and Cora Lee Howell
Tom and Carmella Intihar
Jennie Intrieri and Family
Sam and Doris Jean Intrieri
Jake and Eleanor Jacobs
Dick and Esther Janacone
  and Family

John and Theresa Jardini and Family
Cecilia Jaros
Jean John
Don and Janet Johnson and Family
Dick and Ruth Jones
Mary Jussek
Father Clarence Karawsky
Bill and Kathy Karazsia and Billy
Jerry and Joanne Kardos
Wayne and Jan Kaufman
Bob and Annette Kelly
Ron and Janet Kelly
Bill and Donna Kepple
Jim and Nancy Kerr
Father Larry Kiniry
Anita Kirkpatrick
Mary Kissel
Sylvester and Shirley Kissel
Marshall and Dorothy Klingensmith
Len and Loretta Kocur and Family
Bob and Joyce Kovalik
Bill and Rose Krafick and Family
Pastor Lee and Linda Kritizer
Lee Krznaric
Pastor Rich and Sally Krznaric
Dr. John Kuth and Family
Chuck and Mary Lalley
Dorothy Lamb
Sister Ann Lazar
Leo and Flo Lekavich and Family
Jenny Locorotondo
Bob and Marie Lucas
John and Ida Lucas and Family
Pauline Lucas
Dr. Bill Lundie
Bob and Joan McDermott
Maxine McQuaide
Bill and Irene McGinley
Raymond and Josephine Maffeo
Angeline Maglocci
Frank and Martha Maglocci
  and Family
James and Goldie Maglocci
  and Family
Milly Maglocci
Pete Maglocci
Rose Majeran and Family
Sister Christine Makowski
Sister Julie Makowski
Adeline Maraffi
Patty Marietto
Delores Marincik
Leo and Rose Marseli

Josephine Martier
Rose and Lenora Martier
Sister Benita Matters
Sister Elizabeth Matz
Bill Mendicino
Sam and Peg Mendicino and Family
Bill and Chris Michaels
Lou and Peg Milie
Bob and Mary Miller and Family
Danny Miller
Mary Miller
Rose Miller
George and Connie Mistrick
Sam and Rita Moliterno and Family
Tony and Josephine Moliterno
and Family
Ray and Michelle Montgomery
Pastor Sheldon and Connie Moore
Ben and Jean Mordadei
Elaine Morroco
Herman and B.J. Mortor
John and Mary Murray and Family
Rev. Rod and Jerri Murray
Andy and Dot Musala
Jenny Musial and Annette
Ellie Myers
Bill and Phil Naccarato and Family
Mary Naccarato
Gabrielli Nastuck
Dave and Judy Nelson and Family
Janie Nelson
Sister Norma
Frank and Debra Notarnicola
and Family
Lucy Odasso
Silvio and Ellen Odasso and Family
Virginia Osol
Patsy and Betty Palatella
Nick and Christine Palucacos
Tom and Julie Palucacos
Louis and Evelyn Pangrazi
and Family
Ismina Pantta
Larry and Patti Pecko and Family
Mary Pellegrino
James Peterman
Caroline Perrino
Joseph and Madelyn Petrarca
Mark and Cheryl Piper
Carmen and Sue Policicchio
and Family
Father Luke Policicchio
Urban and Jean Policicchio

Alma Polka
Tim and Charleen Polka
Jack and Jean Poti
Dave and Martha Predajna
Michael and Susan Protz and Family

Dr. and Mrs. August Pugliese
and Family
Guida Pugliese and Family
Lil Pugliese and Family
Mary Rametta and Family
Sylvia Ravotti
Fran and Dee Raymond and Family
Lucy Recchi
Sister Bridget Reilly
Isabel Rendek and Family
Sam and Carole Reo and Family
Mary Rielly
Rosalind Riley
Bud and Glenna Mae Risher
and Family
Doug and Regina Risher and Family
Nate and Carmella Roberto
and Family
Jimmie and Milly Rock
Mary Rojeski
Jack Rubin and Family
Donna Rumbaugh
Joe and Pauline Rykaceski
Pauline Saben and Family
Dr. Hal and Nina Samay and Family
Tom Sanders
Angelina Scalzott
Don and Marilyn Scalzott and Family
Jane Scott
Dick and Leona Sebastian
and Family
Victor and Rose Sebastian
Don and Marsha Sgarleta and Family
John and Jeanne Shaffer
Sandy Shuster
Frank and Josephine Silvestri
Frank and Olga Silvestri
Josephine Silvestri
Tony and Louise Silware and Family
Adale Sluka
Dr. Tim Sluser
Bob and Carmella Smith
Pearl Snyder
Betty Solomon and Family
Leona Soltis and Family
Kim Stover

Lillian Straka
Marion Straka
Ruth Sulava
Annette and Stacy Szuch
Ann Stone and Family
Gene and Mary Jane Swiderek
Jim Szymanski
Pastor John and Linda Szymanski
Stan and Rose Szymanski
    and Family
Stan and Mary Tarosky and Family
John and Jerry Toncini and Family
Mary Jo Traficanto
Don Traister
Terri Trawenski and Family
Joe and Dorothy Trentin
Larry and Gloria Trentin
Louise Trentin
Crissy Troilo
Nick and Norma Troilo
Andy and Barb Uncapher
Milton and Barb Uncapher
Al and Julie Uskuraitis and Family
Joe and Marie Valentino
Mary Vecchio and Family
Albert and Adeline Vellucci
Richard and Domenica Venturini
Edna Vespa and Family
Andy and Jean Vida
Rich and Jeri Vidunas
Steve and Kathy Vonderach
    and Family
Steve and Sophie Vonderach
Stan and Nellie Waikus
James and Mary Lee Walker
Pastor Tom and Debbie Walters
Russ and Lee White
Mr. and Mrs. Glen Watterson
Jim and Peggy Wien
Pastor Phil Williams
Henry and Vi Wojcik and Family
Mary Ann Wyscik
Mary Yacura
Arlene Young and Family
Tony and Mary Lynn Zacklene
    and Family
Ann Zelonka
Dr. Michael Zernich

PHYSICIANS

Dr. Judy Figura
Dr. Jack Hill
Dr. William Lundie
Dr. David G. Mayernik
Dr. Teresa A. Nolan
Dr. Donald Reigal
Dr. Charles Srodes

NURSING STAFF

Nancy Barron
Sue Beikman
Elaine Bowser
Kathy Callihan
Laura Cato
Georgia Coleman
Sue Cromeams
Lori Maier Ellis
Joyce Fischer
Barb Kelly
Michell Kemper
Carmen King
Kim Lamb
Carol Larkin
Patty McCaffrey

Sandy Malone
Pat Marshall
Janet Mullen
Cathy Peretic
Carole Pore
Isabel Posey
Dawn Read
Lisa Zolocsik Romani
Angela Stovenec
Beth Murphy Superdoc
Denise Uhran
Regina Verecilla
Sarah Wilson White
Denise Youghen
Michelle Zimmerman

FOOD SERVICE WORKER

Shirley Turner

SOCIAL WORKER

Sue Mull

HOUSEKEEPING

Leslie Salerno

TRANSPORTS

Judi Haslage
Elizabeth Jenkins
Ida Scott

INTRAVENOUS (I.V.) TEAM

Sally Allison
Maureen Blair
Pat Foreman
Nancy Honess
Sylvia Kahan
Kay Kerr
Mickey King
Sue Klann
Darrell Lis
Bonita Lofts
Bob McCollum
Winnie Marsh
Bernie Smith
Mary Swartz
Ken Vignevic